Except for Fornication

The Teaching of the Lord Jesus on Divorce and Remarriage

By H. Van Dyke Parunak

Energion Publications
P. O. Box 841
Gonzalez, FL 32560

www.energionpubs.com

2011

Cover Design: Jason Neufeld (jasonneufelddesign.com)

ISBN10: 1-893729-94-X
ISBN13: 978-1893729-94-0
Library of Congress Control Number: 2011938663

TABLE OF CONTENTS

From the Editors...v

Preface..vii

1 Matthew's Puzzle.. 1

2 The Law of Moses and Fornication................................. 17

3 The Law of Moses and Divorce.....................................29

4 Our Lord Corrects Jewish Errors.................................. 41

5 Paul's Teaching on Divorce...53

6 God Knows the Way Out... 63

Appendix 1: Methodological Notes.................................. 69

Appendix 2: What Is Fornication?................................... 73

Bibliography...79

Topics and Persons Index..81

Scripture Index...83

FROM THE EDITORS

The Areopagus is a hill in Athens that was once the meeting place of a Greek council. Paul preached on that hill while visiting Athens, presenting the gospel to the Athenian council and converting one of them (Acts 17). It thus provides an excellent name for this series of booklets that examines important issues in understanding Christian beliefs and developing sound Christian practice. Each booklet is intentionally short – less than 80 pages in length – and provides an academically sound and biblically rooted examination of a particular question about doctrine or practice or an area of basic Christian belief.

The Areopagus series is orthodox in doctrine but not bound to the doctrinal statements of any denomination. It is both firm in conviction and irenic in tone. Authors have been chosen for their ability to understand a topic in depth and present it clearly.

Each book is rigorous in scholarship because we believe the church deserves no less. Yet the volumes are accessible in style as we also believe that there are many pastors and laypersons in the church who desire to think deeply and critically about the issues that confront the church today in its life and mission in the world.

In keeping with these convictions, the authors in this series are either professors who are also actively involved in ministry, pastors who have not only thought through the issues but whose ministry has been guided by their convictions, or laypersons whose faith and commitment to the lordship of Jesus Christ and his church have contributed to the Great Commission Jesus gave to all of his followers (Matt. 28:18-20).

The Areopagus Critical Christian Issues series is not only meant to help the church think differently. We hope that those who read its volumes will be different, for the gospel is about the transformation of the whole person – mind, heart, and soul.

We take the words of the apostle Paul seriously when he says to the Athenians that God "has fixed a day on which he will have the world judged in righteousness by a man whom he has appointed; and of this he has given assurance to all by raising him from the dead" (Acts 17:31).

Allan R. Bevere
David Alan Black
Editors

PREFACE

"Tell me why you want to write this book."

My wife Anita asks the most probing questions. Thirty years ago, she encouraged me to write down our understanding of the Bible's teaching on divorce and remarriage. She spent endless hours corresponding with publishers, collecting nothing but terse rejections. She shared my excitement when Energion expressed interest in publishing a short volume based on the material. Then, as we began to plan our schedule to make time for the revision, she turned to me and asked,

"Tell me why you want to write this book."

I've been thinking about that question. I realize that two things prompted me to write this book: I fear God, and I love my Christian brothers and sisters.

My fear of God motivates me because of James' warning,

My brethren, be not many teachers, knowing that we shall receive the greater judgment (James 3:1).

God will hold me accountable for what I teach others. Long ago, a wise Bible teacher counseled me and other young men who hoped to serve the church of God, "Be sure to figure out in advance what you believe about divorce and remarriage. Sooner or later, you will have to counsel people who are embroiled in this tragic situation. It's far better that you figure out what you believe now, while you can be objective with the Scriptures, than when you are deeply immersed in the emotional trauma of those you love." My sense of the serious responsibility of teaching, and my need to stand before God and give an account, has led me to invest many hours in understanding the biblical position as accurately as I can.

Of course, I could avoid this burden by avoiding the topic, but my love for you won't let me. The tragedy of divorce and remarriage touches everybody in today's culture. My brothers and sisters are hurting. I see them acting in ways that will make them unhappy, and ultimately bring God's chastisement on them. How can I stay silent?

So the fear of God, and my love for his people, have led me to study this issue, and present it in a way that I hope will be clear and helpful to you.

Personal holiness matters. While our salvation is by grace through faith and apart from works (Eph 2:8-9), God's purpose in saving us is that we should walk in good works (Eph 2:10). The God who reveals himself in the Bible is unspeakably holy. Even the exalted angels have to repeat themselves to describe his holiness (Isa 6:3). As our Creator, he has absolute authority over us. He has revealed his will to us, and holds us accountable to obey it.

None of us can obey God's law in our own strength. We've all sinned, and come short of God's glory (Rom 6:23). So he has sent his Son to bear his wrath against our sin, and to rise again to prove that he has broken the power of our sin.

It is a blessing beyond telling to know that my sins are forgiven, that I stand before God accepted in his beloved Son. His Spirit gives me a desire to live according to his word, so I must understand what that word teaches. Holiness is not optional. The same New Testament that tells how God has accepted me, and promises eternal life to all who believe, also reminds me, "Without [holiness] no man shall see the Lord" (Heb 12:14). It tells me that it is a fearful thing to fall into the hands of the living God (Heb 10:31), and warns that those who disobey God's law shall not inherit his kingdom (1 Cor 6:9-10). In today's culture, issues surrounding divorce and remarriage are at the forefront of the challenges to those who would please the Lord. This book is my gift to the Lord, and to you, in an effort to help with this challenge.

I'd like you to share my experience of discovery as I studied this subject. So I have organized the book as a mystery. I start with some puzzles and contradictions, next introduce evidence that can help solve them, and then tie the pieces together. If you like to read mysteries starting with the conclusion, you can turn directly to Chapter 4. But if you start at the beginning, perhaps you can share the excitement of figuring out the answer yourself.

This volume focuses on our Lord's teaching about divorce and remarriage in the Gospels. It is drawn from a much longer study that covers the entire Bible. In this volume, I will sometimes refer to that study as "the longer book." That work offers more technical detail on the passages considered in this volume, and also discusses the pastoral implications of how to deal with cases of divorce and remarriage in the modern church. It is available as a free e-book at:

http://www.cyber-chapel.org/DivorceAndRemarriage

I am deeply indebted to many brothers and sisters who have encouraged me in pursuing this study. The Bible teacher mentioned above, whose name I have forgotten, is among them. My late father-in-law, Dr. Gene Nowlin, stimulated my thinking four decades ago when he asked how one could reconcile the apparent permission of divorce in Deuteronomy 24:1 with the Lord's teaching in the Gospels. The preface to the longer book acknowledges those who carefully reviewed it. Many portions that they helped improve are part of the present work. I am grateful to James Lee for suggesting Energion as a publisher, and to Henry Neufeld for encouraging the work and making it available in this form to a broader audience. My wife Anita led the review effort on this version with her detailed comments and her repeated requests for clarity. Karl and Valerie Gross, Rick and Ginny Gross, Ross Leavitt, James and Rachel Lee, Dave and Sandy Nelson, and Gene and Andrea Parunak reviewed the text and offered suggestions. If you can understand what I've written, join me in thanking God for them. If you can't, it's my fault, but if you contact me via the publisher or the web site above, I'll do my best to clarify.

H. Van Dyke Parunak
Ann Arbor, MI

1
MATTHEW'S PUZZLE

Four times in the Gospels, on three separate occasions, the Lord Jesus teaches about divorce and remarriage: Matthew 5:31-32; 19:9; Mark 10:10-12; and Luke 16:17-18. Most of these teachings are very similar. In each case he is responding to the conventional Jewish teaching, which permits divorce and remarriage. Our Lord consistently teaches that remarriage after divorce is adultery: for the divorced wife (Matt 5), the divorcing husband (Matt 19, Mark 10, Luke 16), the woman's second husband (Matt 5, Matt 19, Luke 16), and even a woman who initiates a divorce (Mark 10).

There is one major distinction among these passages. In Matthew, and only in Matthew, the Lord makes an exception for fornication.

> *Furthermore it has been said,*
> > *"Whoever dismisses his wife, let him give her*
> > *a divorce."*
> *But I say to you that whoever dismisses his wife,*
> > ***except for the cause of fornication,***
> > *causes her to commit adultery,*
> *and whoever marries a dismissed woman*
> > *commits adultery.*   Matthew 5:31-32

> *Whoever dismisses his wife,*
> > ***except for fornication,***
> > *and marries another,*
> > *commits adultery,*

> *and he who marries a dismissed woman*
> *commits adultery.*   Matthew 19:9

Understanding this exception is the main focus of this book.

Both of these texts discuss ending one marriage and entering into another. Both of them contain the words "except for [the cause of] fornication." In this so-called "fornication clause," the Lord authorizes the husband to "dismiss" his wife if she is guilty of fornication. (Fornication is intimacy between two people who are not married to each other. Appendix 2 studies the meaning of fornication and its relation to adultery in more detail.)

What does it mean for a man to dismiss his wife? Many people think these verses are speaking about divorce. Those who hold this position usually go on to authorize remarriage after such a divorce. This position goes back to the Dutch scholar Erasmus of Rotterdam, who lived around 1500, so we will call it "Erasmus' view." It is embodied in the Westminster Confession of Faith (1646):

> Adultery or fornication committed after a contract, being detected before marriage, giveth just occasion to the innocent party to dissolve that contract. In the case of adultery after marriage, it is lawful for the innocent party to sue out a divorce: and after the divorce, to marry another, as if the offending party were dead (Westminster Confession, 24.5).

Many Christians hold this view today. However, if we read Matthew carefully with the view that the Lord is authorizing divorce, we will be puzzled. In fact, we will be puzzled in three ways. Let me share these puzzles with you.

A PUZZLE WITHIN THE VERSES

Erasmus' view of the fornication clause leads to contradictions within the verses in which the clause appears. In Matthew

19:9 Erasmus allows the husband to remarry, and in Matthew 5:32 he allows the wife to remarry, but both verses say that any future spouse of the wife is guilty of adultery. If it's not wrong for members of the original couple to remarry, why is the second marriage wrong for the husband in the wife's second marriage?

To understand this puzzle, let's work through an example. Andy and Ann are husband and wife. Ann becomes unfaithful to Andy. What may they do now?

> *But I say to you that whoever dismisses his wife,*
> **except for the cause of fornication,**
> *causes her to commit adultery.*   Matthew 5:32

This verse answers two questions that Ann and Andy may have:

1. May Andy divorce Ann?
2. May Ann remarry?

Both answers depend on the words "causes her to commit adultery." These words are most naturally understood to say that if a man dismisses his wife, she will be likely to remarry, and in so doing would commit adultery. The temptation for her to remarry is particularly great in a culture (like that of Judea in the first century) in which women have little economic independence. If there is no fornication, the verse teaches that a man who dismisses his wife puts her in a situation where she must remarry, and thus commit adultery. The wife sins in remarrying, and the husband sins by causing her to stumble. Without fornication, the answer to our two questions is clearly "No," regardless of whether we follow Erasmus or not.

The fornication clause says that fornication somehow removes these concerns. The presence of fornication allows Andy to dismiss Ann without causing her to commit adultery. Since Erasmus understands "dismiss" to mean "divorce," he would also counsel Ann that, once divorced because of fornication, she can remarry without being guilty of adultery.

Some will object, "This is unfair! If Andy divorces Ann without just cause, Ann is *not* free to remarry, but if Ann commits fornication, she *is* free to remarry. Such a teaching would encourage a woman in a rocky marriage to commit fornication so that, if her husband divorces her, she can at least marry another husband." Erasmus' position does indeed lead to this conclusion. For now, we are concerned with what the text says, not whether we find the teaching fair. Our final solution will avoid this injustice.

In the case of fornication, Erasmus answers "Yes" to both question 1 and question 2.

Now we turn to the first sentence of Matthew 19:9.

> *Whoever dismisses his wife,*
> **except for fornication,**
> *and marries another,*
> *commits adultery.*   Matthew 19:9a

This sentence raises a third question in Andy's mind.

3.   May Andy remarry after he divorces Ann?

If there is no fornication, the answer to this question is clearly "No" (again, whether we agree with Erasmus or not). In fact, the teaching in Mark (part of the same setting as Matthew 19, but a different utterance), says this directly without mentioning fornication:

> *Whoever dismisses his wife,*
> *and marries another,*
> *commits adultery against her.*

> Mark 10:11

But the fornication clause in Matthew 19:9 says that if there has been fornication, Andy may remarry without being guilty of adultery. So, according to Erasmus, the answer to question 3 is also "Yes."

So far, everything is consistent. Based on the answer to question 1, Andy divorces Ann. Based on the answer to question 3, he later marries Betty. Meanwhile, Ann falls in love with Bob.

Based on the answer to question 2, they begin to discuss marriage.

Bob isn't completely comfortable. He understands that, according to Erasmus, Ann is free to remarry (question 2). But he wonders whether *he* is free to marry *her*. This is a separate question:

4. May another man marry Ann?

What troubles him is the second sentence in each of the Lord's teachings in Matthew, and also in Luke.

> *Whoever marries a dismissed woman commits adultery.*   Matthew 5:32

> *He who marries a dismissed woman commits adultery.*
>   Matthew 19:9

> *Every one marrying a woman dismissed from a husband commits adultery.*   Luke 16:18

None of these sentences says anything about fornication. Imagine that Erasmus comes back to help Bob sort things out. Bob asks Erasmus, "How come it's all right for Ann to marry me (question 2), but not for me to marry Ann (question 4)? If we're married to each other, how can one of us be guilty of adultery, while the other is not ?"

Erasmus replies, "Well, the fornication clause authorizes Ann's divorce, and leaves her free to remarry. Logically, that must mean that her future spouse is free to remarry, too."

Bob isn't so sure. "But the Lord makes no exception in the sentences that talk about my marrying Ann," he points out. "It only occurs in the sentence that talks about her marrying me."

"I know," replies Erasmus, "but logically, the Lord must have meant the fornication clause to apply to both parts of Matthew 5:30-32 and 19:9. Otherwise the second sentence contradicts the first one."

"If that's what he meant," Bob asks, "why didn't he say it that way?"

Bob is well to be cautious. Erasmus' attempt to extend the fornication clause to the warning not to marry a dismissed woman may sound logical, but it is without any justification from the text. Let's look at Matthew's verses a little more closely.

Each verse consists of two parallel statements. In 5:32, these are:

1. *Whoever dismisses his wife, except for the cause of fornication, causes her to commit adultery, and*
2. *whoever marries a dismissed woman commits adultery.*

In 19:9, they are

1. *Whoever dismisses his wife, except for fornication, and marries another, commits adultery, and*
2. *he who marries a dismissed woman commits adultery.*

The fornication clause comes in the middle of the first statement, and thus modifies only that statement. Our Lord could have repeated the fornication clause in each of the two sentences. For example, in Matthew 5:31-32, he could have said,

1. *Whoever dismisses his wife, except for the cause of fornication, causes her to commit adultery, and*
2. *whoever marries a dismissed woman, except for the cause of fornication, commits adultery.*

That arrangement would mean that fornication justifies both dismissing and remarriage. If the Lord had repeated the clause, Bob would be comfortable marrying Ann. But the Lord didn't repeat it.

Alternatively, the Lord could have uttered the fornication clause before the first of the two clauses, like this (again using Matthew 5:31-32 for concreteness),

*I say to you that, **except for the cause of fornication**,*

1. *Whoever dismisses his wife causes her to commit adultery, and*

2. *whoever marries a dismissed woman commits adultery.*

This arrangement wouldn't be quite as clear as the first, but would at least open up the possibility that the exception applies to the second statement as well as the first.

The Lord didn't do either of these things. By putting the fornication clause in the middle of the first statement, he clearly limits it only to the first statement. There is no grammatical justification for applying it to the second statement. Bob realizes this, and calls off his relation with Ann.

If fornication ends Ann's marriage to Andy and allows her to marry Bob without committing adultery, why doesn't it allow Bob to marry her? Erasmus' explanation leaves a huge puzzle, right within Matthew's verses.

A PUZZLE WITH THE LOCAL CONTEXT

Erasmus' view of the fornication clause leads to a puzzle in the individual verses where it occurs. It also leads to a puzzle with the setting of each verse.

Let's start with Matthew 5:32. This verse comes in the middle of a series of six contrasts, summarized in Table 1. In each contrast, the Lord corrects a teaching that is already in circulation. People sometimes suggest that the teachings are Old Testament principles that the Lord is replacing with new instruction. He is doing no such thing. He introduces this section by affirming his commitment to the Old Testament law:

> *Do not think that I came to destroy the Law or the Prophets. I did not come to destroy but to fulfill. For assuredly, I say to you, until heaven and earth pass away, one jot or one tittle will by no means pass from the Law until all comes to pass. Whoever therefore loosens one of the least of these commandments, and teaches men so, shall be called least in the kingdom of heaven; but whoever does and teaches them, he shall be called*

Table 1: The Contrasts of Matthew 5

Murder	(5:21) *You have heard that it was said to those of old, "You shall not murder; and whoever murders will be in danger of the judgment."*	(5:22-26) *But I say to you that whoever is angry with his brother without a cause shall be in danger of the judgment. …*
Adultery	(5:27) *You have heard that it was said to those of old, "You shall not commit adultery."*	(5:28-30) *But I say to you that whoever looks at a woman to lust for her has already committed adultery with her in his heart. …*
Divorce	(5:31) *Furthermore it has been said, "Whoever dismisses his wife, let him give her a divorce."*	(5:32) *But I say to you that whoever dismisses his wife, except for the cause of fornication, causes her to commit adultery; and whoever marries a dismissed woman commits adultery.*
Oaths	(5:33) *Again you have heard that it was said to those of old, "You shall not swear falsely, but shall perform your oaths to the Lord."*	(5:34-37) *But I say to you not to swear at all, …*
Revenge	(5:38) *You have heard that it was said, "An eye for an eye and a tooth for a tooth."*	(5:39-42) *But I say to you not to resist an evil person. But whoever slaps you on your right cheek, turn the other to him also. …*
Love	(5:43) *You have heard that it was said, "You shall love your neighbor and hate your enemy."*	(5:44-48) *But I say to you, "Love your enemies, …"*

great in the kingdom of heaven. For I say to you, that unless your righteousness exceeds that of the scribes and Pharisees, you will by no means enter the kingdom of heaven (Matt 5:17-20).

The last verse of this introduction, Matthew 5:20, shows the real source of the erroneous teachings. They represent the *"righteousness ... of the scribes and Pharisees,"* the Jewish tradition in the first century. The summaries of their teaching sound like the Old Testament because these religious leaders quote the Old Testament, but they alter it or take it out of context, deviating from the original intent. The Lord is calling them back to the true sense of the Old Testament.

The error that the Lord is correcting in the third pair is *"Whoever dismisses his wife, let him give her a divorce."* The Jewish teachers of the first century permit divorce and remarriage, but disagree about what kind of behavior justifies a divorce. One party, the school of Hillel, allows a man to divorce his wife for any cause. The other, the school of Shammai, allows divorce only for a grave offense, such as adultery. Both parties agree that divorce is possible, and this agreement is the error that the Lord is correcting. Yet, according to Erasmus, the Lord is not challenging *"the righteousness of the scribes and Pharisees,"* but is simply siding with Shammai against Hillel. If his words simply agree with Shammai, he is blunting his condemnation of rabbinical teaching.

Taking sides in this rabbinical debate would be fatal to the Lord's argument in Matthew 19:9 as well. Let's recall the setting of this teaching. The Lord is making his way south from Galilee to Jerusalem. His route leads down the eastern bank of the Jordan river, through the territory called Perea. Perea is ruled by Herod Antipas, who beheaded John the Baptist as the final act in a drama that began when John spoke out against Antipas' marriage to a divorced woman (Mark 6:17-28). The Pharisees know that divorce is a sensitive subject in Perea. They suspect that the Lord's position on divorce is similar to John's. When they find

Christ in Herod's territory, they try to lure him into a statement that will enrage Herod's wife, so that she will destroy him as she did John.

They lay their trap by inviting him to comment on the classic disagreement between Hillel and Shammai. In 19:3, they ask,

Is it lawful for a man to dismiss his wife for any cause?

Hillel would answer, "Yes." Shammai would respond, "No, only for gross misbehavior." Their strategy is the same as in Matthew 22:16-17, where a group including both Pharisees (who want Jewish independence) and Herodians (who approve of Herod's Roman patrons) asks him whether it is lawful to pay the poll tax to Caesar. In both cases, either answer will ingratiate him to one party, while alienating the other. The Lord refuses to take sides. The question is not which party he endorses, but whether they will endorse him as the Messiah.

Even with his followers, the Lord refuses to act as referee. To one who asks him to settle a question of inheritance, he replies (Luke 12:13, 14), *"Who made me a judge or arbitrator over you?"* The debate is of the same form in Matthew 19. The Pharisees want him to side with one or the other of the dominant positions. The Lord rejects both of their arguments.

> *He, answering, said to them, "Have you not read, that he who made them at the beginning made them male and female, 5 And said, 'For this cause shall a man leave father and mother, and shall cleave to his wife: and they two shall become one flesh?' 6 Wherefore they are no more two, but one flesh. What therefore God has joined together, let not man separate"* (Matt 19:4-6).

At this point in the discussion, the Lord's response is clear, and consistent with his policy in Matthew 22 concerning the poll tax. He condemns both of the parties that seek his endorsement. They want to debate over which offenses do or do not justify divorce. He responds that divorce itself is contrary to the instruction in Genesis.

When we get to verse 9, though, the Lord says to the Pharisees,

> Whoever dismisses his wife, **except for fornication,** and marries another, commits adultery.

If Erasmus is right, this statement reverses the Lord's teaching in verses 4-6. Erasmus' understanding of this verse takes the side of Shammai. Such a reversal would be unprecedented among the recorded interviews of our Lord with his adversaries.

A PUZZLE WITH THE OTHER GOSPELS

The first puzzle resulting from Erasmus' understanding of the fornication clause is in the logic of the individual verses in which it appears. The second puzzle is the contradiction it causes with the context of each of these verses. Now, let's consider the third puzzle, involving inconsistency across the different Gospels.

Mark and Luke, like Matthew, consider the case of a man's divorcing his wife. According to Erasmus, Matthew 19:9 allows the man to remarry if the divorce is the result of fornication. Mark and Luke do not. Their prohibition of remarriage is absolute. Table 2 compares all four passages.

It is particularly interesting to compare Matthew 19 with Mark 10, because the Lord gives both of these teachings during the same sequence of events.

Matthew's statement records part of the Lord's response to the Pharisees. Afterward, the disciples privately express surprise at the harshness of his position. The Lord repeats to them in private what he told the Pharisees in public. Matthew 19:9 is the public statement to the Pharisees, while Mark 10:11-12 is the private repetition to the disciples.

Mark has arranged his material so that the answer to the question "Is divorce lawful?" is a clear and simple "No." If Erasmus is right, then the Lord's public teaching (recorded in Matthew) contradicts what he told the disciples privately (recorded in

Table 2: Comparing the Lord's Four Teachings

Matt 5:32	Matt 19:9	Mark 10:11-12	Luke 16:18
Whoever dismisses his wife,	*Whoever dismisses his wife,*	*Whoever dismisses his wife,*	*Every one dismissing his wife*
except for the cause of fornication	*except for fornication*		
causes her to commit adultery;			
	and marries another, commits adultery,	*and marries another, commits adultery against her,*	*and marrying another commits adultery;*
and whoever marries a dismissed woman commits adultery.	*and he who marries a dismissed woman commits adultery.*		*and every one marrying a woman dismissed from a husband commits adultery.*
		and if a woman dismisses her husband and is married to another, she commits adultery.	

Mark). It also contradicts his teaching in Luke, which took place in a different setting from any of the other divorce sayings.

Erasmus would no doubt insist that the Gospels must be treated as a unit. He would expect us to read Mark and Luke while keeping in mind what Matthew wrote. This assumption is a larger-scale version of the assumption that the fornication clause in the first sentence of Matthew 5:32 and 19:9 should be applied to the second sentence of each verse. Now we are asked to assume that the influence of the clause should be carried from one book to another.

In modern Bibles, all four Gospels are bound as a single book. Center references enable us to flip quickly from a verse in one Gospel to a parallel verse in another. It is easy for us to carry over ideas from one Gospel to another. Our modern experience with a single Bible encourages people to assume that a qualification stated in one Gospel should be understood to apply to the others as well.

But the Gospels have not always been part of a single book. When they were first written, they were not bound together. Each was a separate book. They were written for different audiences, at different times, and in different places. Scholars debate whether the author of one Gospel may have had access to an earlier one, or whether two Gospels sometimes share a common source that is no longer preserved. We do not need to resolve these questions, but simply observe that the Gospels existed independently before they were bound together. Each was respected as the Word of God in the assemblies of believers where it was available. Initially, no single assembly had all four Gospels. As a result, each assembly's record of the Lord's teaching may have been *incomplete* (as ours is today, according to John 21:25). But if we accept each of the Gospels as inspired, we must conclude that no assembly's record was *incorrect*.

For example, let's imagine that a Christian assembly in city A has a copy of Matthew, while Mark's Gospel is circulating in city B. Let's look again at Andy and Ann. Andy divorces Ann, then comes to the elders in his assembly and asks whether he may marry Betty. If Erasmus is correct, Andy will receive opposite answers, depending on whether he happens to live in city A or city B. The elders in city A, reading Matthew, will say, "Yes, you may remarry." The elders in city B, reading Mark, will say, "No you may not." This difference shows that, as they were originally written, Erasmus' interpretation makes Matthew contradict Mark. In fact, there is no evidence that the early church split along lines such as these. The early church fathers did not allow remarriage, regardless of the cause of the divorce, whether they were reading Matthew, Mark, or Luke. The evidence is conveniently summarized by Heth and Wenham 1984. Even in the third century, by which time the gospels were routinely read together, the fathers still did not use the exception from Matthew to color their understanding of Mark and Luke.

WHERE DO WE GO NOW?

Erasmus' understanding of the fornication clause leads to three puzzles: one within the individual verses where the clause appears, a second between these verses and their immediate context, and a third across the different Gospels. Confusion like this in studying the Bible usually indicates an incorrect understanding. It's a warning to look again, more closely, before using Matthew 5:32 and 19:9 to justify such serious actions as divorce and remarriage.

To avoid these contradictions, those who agree with Erasmus must make ungrammatical assumptions. Several alternative views, reviewed in the longer book, have been proposed, but they are hardly convincing. There must be a better solution.

I believe that there is.

Two passages in the Law of Moses lie behind the Lord's teaching on divorce and remarriage. Deuteronomy 22 deals with the consequences of impurity in marriage. Deuteronomy 24 regulates divorce. As we study these passages, we must keep in mind the Lord's words in Matthew 5:17-20:

Do not think that I came to destroy the Law or the Prophets. I did not come to destroy but to fulfill. For assuredly, I say to you, until heaven and earth pass away, one jot or one tittle will by no means pass from the Law until all comes to pass. Whoever therefore loosens one of the least of these commandments, and teaches men so, shall be called least in the kingdom of heaven; but whoever does and teaches them, he shall be called great in the kingdom of heaven. For I say to you, that unless your righteousness exceeds that of the scribes and Pharisees, you will by no means enter the kingdom of heaven.

He makes two points. First, he does not relax Moses' law, but endorses every detail of it. Second, he condemns the religious leaders of his day for falling short of this standard. When we understand what the law requires and how the Jews of the first century were compromising it, we will be able to understand our Lord's teaching on divorce and remarriage.

2

THE LAW OF MOSES AND FORNICATION

Our Lord claims that his teaching about marriage, including the fornication clause, reinforces the law of Moses. The law of Moses is not silent on the subject of fornication. Deuteronomy 22:13-29 brings together many warnings against this sin.

A modern book of non-fiction, such as a textbook, uses a variety of devices (including a table of contents, bold-faced headings, indentation, and different sizes of type) to show how the material is organized. These devices do not appear in ancient books. Instead, symmetrical patterns of repetition show where sections begin and end, and indicate their inner structure. Deuteronomy 22 is an excellent example of this technique.

- We begin by **surveying** the structure of the section that discusses fornication.
- When we understand this structure, we can study each law in **detail.**
- We summarize **two principles** that we learn from the passage.
- Finally, we discuss the status of this law **in our Lord's day**.

SURVEY OF DEUTERONOMY 22:13-29

Deuteronomy 22:13-29 contains five main laws, beginning at verses 13, 22, 23, 25, and 28. Each law begins with the words

"If a man ... " or "If a damsel ... ," and discusses three points:

1. the marital status of the woman;
2. an illicit physical union between the woman and some man, in which the man is always guilty and the woman is sometimes innocent and sometimes guilty;
3. the consequences for the woman (and the man, if he can be identified).

The order of the points varies from law to law, and sometimes the second point is assumed rather than stated, but the recurrence of the three main themes is remarkable. To make these ideas clear, we print the text with notes along the side identifying the words and phrases that show the woman's status, her guilt or innocence, and the consequences.

First Paragraph, verses 13-21:

1. Woman married	*If a man takes a wife and goes in unto her, and hates her, and lodges irresponsible charges, and brings up an evil name upon her, and says, "I took this woman, and when I came to her, I did not find that she had tokens of virginity,"*
2. Woman innocent	*then the father of the damsel and her mother shall take and bring out the tokens of the damsel's virginity to the elders of the city in the gate. The damsel's father shall say to the elders, "I gave my daughter to this man as a wife, and he hates her, and look, he has lodged irresponsible charges." ...*
3. Consequence	*Then the elders of that city shall take that man and chastise him, and they shall fine him a hundred shekels of silver, and shall give them to the father of the damsel, ... and she shall be his wife. He may not put her away all his days .*

2. Woman guilty	*But if this thing is true, and the tokens of virginity* **are not found** *for the damsel,*
3. Consequence	**then they shall bring out the damsel to the door of her father's house, and the men of her city shall stone her with stones , so that she dies**, *... and you shall put the evil away from among you.*

Second Paragraph, verse 22:

1. Woman married	*If a man is found lying with* **a woman married to a husband ,**
3. Consequence	*then* **both of them shall die**, *both the man who lay with the woman, and the woman, and you shall put away the evil from Israel.*

Third Paragraph, verses 23-24:

1. Woman engaged	**If a damsel** *who is a virgin is betrothed to a man, and a man finds her in the city, and lies with her,*
3. Consequence	*then you shall bring them both out to the gate of that city, and* **you shall stone them with stones, so that they die ,**
2. Woman presumed guilty	*the damsel,* **because she cried not** *, being in the city, and the man, because he has humbled his neighbor's wife, and you shall put away the evil from among you.*

Fourth Paragraph, verses 25-27:

1. Woman engaged	*But if a man finds a **betrothed damsel** in the field, and the man forces her, and lies with her,*
3. Consequence	*then only **the man** who lay with her shall die. **Unto the damsel you shall do nothing** .*
2. Woman innocent	*There is in the damsel **no sin worthy of death.** ... For he found her in the field, and the betrothed damsel cried, and there was none to save her.*

Fifth Paragraph, verses 28-29:

1. Woman single	*If a man finds a damsel who is a virgin, **who is not betrothed** , and lays hold on her, and lies with her, and they are found,*
3. Consequence	*then the man who lay with her **shall give** the damsel's father fifty shekels of silver, and she shall be his wife. Because he has humbled her, **he may not put her away all his days** .*

Table 3 on page 21 summarizes the repeated themes across these five paragraphs.

A Detailed Look at Each Law

Now that we see how these laws are organized, we look at each of them in more detail. The penalties are very severe, but they show how abhorrent impurity is to the Lord.

Table 3: Summary of Deuteronomy 22:13-29

Section	Woman's Status	Woman Guilty?	Consequences
22:13-21 The Wife Accused			
15-19, found innocent	Married	No	Husband fined; may never put her away
20-21, found guilty	Married	Yes	Wife executed by stoning
22:22 The Adulteress Discovered		Not Stated	Wife and illicit partner executed
22:23-24 Defiled in the City	Engaged	Presumed Yes	Man and woman both executed
22:25-27 Defiled in the Country	Engaged	Presumed No	Only man executed; woman goes free
22:28-29 Single Girl Defiled	Single	Not Stated	Man must marry woman; may never put her away

First Paragraph: The Wife Accused, 22:13-21

The first case that Moses discusses is that of a man who accuses his wife of moral impurity before marriage:

> *I took this woman, and when I came to her, I did not*
> *find that she had tokens of virginity* (22:14).

The elders of the city must decide whether the woman is guilty or innocent. They base their decision on the "tokens of virginity" preserved by the wife's parents.

This is the only Bible passage to mention these tokens. Jewish custom of the first few centuries A.D., and much later Arab custom, suggests that they are linens from the nuptial bed, bearing blood stains that show that the husband is the bride's first partner. The marriage feast lasted several days beyond the wedding night, and the sheets were displayed to the guests, then carefully preserved by the bride's parents.

If the parents can produce these cloths, the elders (who would certainly have been present at the marriage feast) are expected to recognize them and pronounce the woman innocent. Then they chastise the man, fine him, and forbid him ever to put away his wife.

If, on the other hand, no one presents the tokens of virginity, the elders declare the woman guilty of the charge, and condemn her to death by stoning. Her death dissolves the union, and the man is free to remarry.

This law says nothing about the man who defiled the woman. It seems unfair to leave him unpunished, while bringing such a harsh judgment on the woman. The other laws make clear that his fate depends on whether the woman was engaged or not at the time he took her. If she was engaged, he is also to be executed (verses 23-27), otherwise not (verses 28-29). The severity of the judgment on the woman reflects, not just her impurity, but her deception in hiding her condition from her fiancé.

Second Paragraph: The Adulteress Discovered, 22:22

When a married woman is discovered with a man who is not her husband, they both die. Their sin is adultery, since the woman is married. There is no question about either what happened, or who the man is, since they are discovered while together.

This is the law invoked by the scribes and Pharisees in John 8:1-11.

The scribes and Pharisees brought to [Jesus] a woman caught in adultery, and when they had set her in the midst, they say to him, "Master, this woman was caught in the act, committing adultery. Moses in the Law commanded us to stone such women. Now: what do you say" (John 8:3-5)?

The Lord points out their own sinfulness, and they slink away, condemned by their own consciences. Then he asks the woman,

"Woman, where are your accusers? Has no one condemned you?" She said, "No one, Lord." Then Jesus said, "Neither do I condemn you. Go, and sin no more" (John 8:10-11).

Moses requires both the man and the woman to die. There is no reason, if they are caught in the act, for only one to be accused. Yet the scribes and Pharisees bring only the woman, not the man, to Jesus. Without both parties, the law cannot be satisfied, even if the scribes stay to press charges. In fact, they abandon the case, and without the witnesses required by Moses (Deut 19:15), even the woman cannot legally be prosecuted. The Lord's actions are completely in keeping with the Law of Moses.

Third Paragraph: Defiled in the City, 22:23-24

An engaged girl attacked in the city is executed, along with her attacker, *"because she cried not."* If she does cry out, she will be acquitted. A person who cries for help in an ancient city can count on being heard. The houses stand close together, often sharing walls, and there is no motor traffic to drown out voices. If people do not learn about the event until later, they will reason, "No one heard her cry, therefore she did not cry, therefore she acquiesced in the sin, therefore she is guilty."

Fourth Paragraph: Defiled in the Country, 22:25-27

If a girl is not heard in the city, the law presumes she is guilty. In the country, she is presumed innocent. Far away from other people, she might well cry out without being heard.

In every section other than this one, the woman is either stoned if guilty (20-21, 22, 23-24) or guaranteed a secure marriage for life if innocent (15-19, 28-29). In this case, the victim is judged innocent, but nothing is said about her coming marriage.

People in Bible times care deeply about family lines and the legitimacy of their children. A man whose fiancée is molested away from the city may well believe that she is innocent, and still not wish to marry her. He might fear that if he did go through with the wedding, people would question who was the real father of his first child. Furthermore, though we understand the law's fairness in assuming that "*the damsel cried, and there was none to save her,*" the husband might be unable to escape a nagging question about her purity in the matter. Moses' law leaves the woman's fate open. She is not to be executed, but she may lose her fiancé.

This paragraph explains Joseph's behavior when Mary "*was found with child of the Holy Spirit*" (Matt 1:18). At first he does not understand the Spirit's role, and can only conclude that she is involved in fornication. Matthew describes him as "*a just man,*" one who lives according to the standards of God's law. The law condemns fornicators to death, yet Joseph resolves "*to put [Mary] away privately,*" and allow her to live. Deuteronomy 22:25-27 lets him spare her life. He assumes that she was forced against her will in the country, and so is innocent. To protect his own family line, he decides "*to put her away.*" He bears her no malice, and so will do this "*privately,*" to spare her the pain of public display. In this case, the Lord protects Mary, by revealing to Joseph the unique nature of her condition, and so Joseph abandons his plans and provides a home for her and the infant Messiah.

Fifth Paragraph: A Single Girl Defiled, 22:28-29

If a man takes a single girl, he must support her for the rest of his life. He is not executed, as he would be if he violated an engaged girl. This difference in his fate points up an interesting contrast in the two situations.

When a man takes an engaged girl (verses 23-27), he seizes one who has been promised to someone else. He wrongs not only the girl, but also her betrothed. The severity of the death penalty reflects the double nature of his sin. A shotgun wedding is out of the question. That would only make his theft of her permanent.

When a man takes an unengaged girl (verses 28-29), he is left alive out of consideration for the girl. If he were stoned, he could not provide a living for her. Furthermore, because of his actions, she may not be able to find another husband. The law spares his life so that he can support her.

"He may not put her away all his days"

In two cases (a man who takes an unengaged maiden, and the husband who wrongly accuses his bride), Moses forbids the husband ever to put away his wife (verses 19 and 29). Some people feel that, because Moses rules out divorce in these situations, he must allow it in other cases.

The Law of Moses contains no global condemnation of divorce. It also contains no blanket approval. The only references it makes to divorce are negative, either forbidding it in specific cases or restricting the behavior of those who have been divorced. However, the prophet Malachi accuses Israel of "*profan[ing] the covenant of our fathers*" (2:10), and backs up his accusation by describing marital abuses, particularly divorce. Malachi clearly sees divorce as contrary to "*the covenant of our fathers,*" which is either the covenant God made with Israel at Mount Sinai through Moses or the earlier covenant with Abraham. Malachi is not reading back New Testament teaching into the Old Testament, and his reference to the Law as the basis for his teaching makes it unlikely that he is suggesting a different standard from that of the Law.

The argument that prohibiting divorce in some situations approves it in all others is only valid if Moses' Law is exhaustive. Clearly, it is not. Deuteronomy 29:29 tells us that it is partial. What it condemns is wrong. What it commands is right. There are some things, including divorce in general, that it neither condemns nor commands. On these subjects we must await the revelation of later Scripture.

TWO IMPORTANT PRINCIPLES

The five laws in Deuteronomy 22:13-29 emphasize two principles that will be important in subsequent chapters.

Why Were Marriages Terminated?

Moses' Law specifies circumstances when a marriage should be terminated. When a man or woman commits adultery, or when an unmarried girl involved in fornication hides her sin from her betrothed until after the wedding, Moses requires an end to the marriage.

The reason for ending the marriage is always moral impurity. There is no mention of "incompatibility," "mental cruelty," or "domestic violence." If a husband accuses his innocent wife, their relationship must be very poor. Still, the Law does not separate them.

The range of impurity in view in Deuteronomy 22:13-29 is extremely broad. It includes premarital affairs, full-fledged adultery after marriage, and infidelity during the engagement period. In Appendix 2, we show that the most natural use of "fornication" is to designate just such a broad array of misbehaviors. In the LXX (the pre-Christian Greek translation of the Old Testament), Deuteronomy 22:13-29 nowhere uses any of the Greek words related to the word "fornication," because it is concerned to distinguish the various specific offenses, not speak in generalities. But in summarizing the misconduct that the chapter describes, "fornication" in its ordinary, general sense would be the perfect word.

How Did the Law Terminate Marriages?

The means by which the Law terminates a marriage is death by stoning. This verdict is very severe, and we may feel squeamish about it, but it shows how terrible fornication is in God's eyes. As severe as it is, it leaves no nagging questions about whether the innocent spouse may remarry. The survivor is not divorced, but widowed. Everyone agrees that in the case of death, the old union is over and done.

Ancient Israel can exact the death penalty for fornication because it is a civil institution as well as a spiritual one. After our Lord's first coming, his people no longer form a worldly kingdom (John 18:36), but are to live under the laws of the various countries in which they live (Rom 13). In western countries, fornication is no longer a capital offense. But under the law of Moses, it was.

HOW DID JEWS HANDLE IMPURITY IN OUR LORD'S DAY?

We observed in Chapter 1 that the Lord Jesus' objective in both Matthew 5 and Matthew 19 is to challenge existing Jewish teachings concerning marriage and divorce. What is the first century practice for dealing with fornication?

The Jewish leaders in the first century acknowledge that the law of Moses requires the death penalty. This understanding is clear in their challenge to the Lord concerning the woman taken in adultery, John 8:2-11. (Whatever one's view of the textual reliability of these verses, there is little question that they reflect the cultural standards of the day.) However, the actual practice during this time is in a state of flux. The Babylonian Talmud is a compendium of Jewish teaching, originally preserved orally, but written down in the first centuries of the Christian era. One passage in it, *Sanhedrin* 41a, states that, forty years before the destruction of the temple, the death penalty ceased to be exacted for any crime. The temple was destroyed in A.D. 70, so the cessation is dated to A.D. 30, the time of the Lord's ministry.

Such a change can hardly have been instantaneous. It must have been a matter of some discussion among the Jews, and the next chapter presents further evidence that the religious elite were moving away from capital punishment. The Babylonian Talmud attributes the end of the death penalty to a change in the meeting place of the Sanhedrin (*Sanhedrin* 41a), but the Mishna (*Makkot* 1:10), an earlier summary of the law, makes it clear that a strong sentiment was growing against the death penalty on the part of many rabbis.

This shift is accompanied by cultural pressure against execution for impurity. Under the Roman *Lex Iulia* promulgated about 17 B.C., the penalty for adultery is divorce, not usually execution. Jews who wish to follow Moses' law would find themselves out of step with their neighbors and possibly in conflict with their Roman governors.

The Pharisees are wavering on the clear and unambiguous penalty prescribed by Deuteronomy 22:13-29 for moral impurity. The Lord Jesus demands a righteousness that exceeds the righteousness of the scribes and Pharisees. They are beginning to neglect God's penalty for fornication. We expect him to call them back to it.

3
THE LAW OF MOSES
AND DIVORCE

In the last chapter we learned that the Old Testament Law, in Deuteronomy 22:13-29, specifies death, not divorce, as the penalty for fornication and adultery. Still, there is divorce in ancient Israel. Twice in four verses, Deuteronomy 24:1-4 describes a man who writes *"a certificate of divorce,"* gives it to his wife, and sends her out of his house.

Since before the time of Christ, interpreters of Deuteronomy 24:1-4 have debated whether or not it sanctions divorce. In this chapter,

– we summarize the **two main views**.
– Then we study four reasons to **prefer** one of these views over the other.
– Finally, we review the understanding of the law **in the first century**.

TWO VIEWS OF DEUTERONOMY 24:1-4

There are two interpretations of Moses' instructions about divorce. One interpretation tells people how to divorce one another. It **authorizes** divorce. The other interpretation recognizes that divorce, like murder and theft, is an unfortunate part of life, and tells people how to behave if it happens. It **takes account of** divorce.

This law, like many in Deuteronomy, has the form, *"If* [or *when*] someone does something, *then* you should do something."

Both interpretations recognize the "if-then" structure of the law. They differ on how many "if-then" statements the law contains.

The translation of Deuteronomy 24:1-4 in the KJV identifies three conditions ("if-then" pairs), followed by an explanation. It sees three laws in the passage, so we call it the "three-law interpretation." Another translation sees only a single instruction and its explanation in the passage. We call it the "one-law interpretation." Table 4 compares the three-law interpretation (on the left) with the one-law interpretation (on the right).

In the three-law interpretation, each of the three conditions is a distinct instruction.

1. The first condition allows a man whose wife does not please him to "*write her a bill of divorcement [a certificate of divorce], and give it in her hand, and send her out of his house*" (verse 1). This law authorizes divorce.
2. The second condition authorizes a divorced woman to marry another man (verse 2).
3. The third condition forbids a woman who is divorced, re-married, and then divorced or widowed to return to the first husband (verses 3-4).

So the three-law interpretation authorizes divorce and remarriage of a woman in whom her husband finds "*some uncleanness.*"

The one-law interpretation recognizes that divorce and remarriage happen, just as Deuteronomy 22:13-29 recognizes that fornication happens. It does not approve the first divorce, or the remarriage, or the second divorce, any more than Deuteronomy 22:13-29 approves fornication. Like Deuteronomy 22:13-29, it tells what God wants people to do if these unfortunate events occur.

CHOOSING BETWEEN THE VIEWS

Four insights show that the one-law interpretation, the one that does not authorize divorce and remarriage, is correct.

Table 4: Two Interpretations of Deut. 24:1-4

Three-Law Interpretation (KJV)	One-Law Interpretation
First Law, 24:1	One Law, 1-4a
When a man hath taken a wife, *and married her,* *and it come to pass*	*When a man has taken a wife,* *and married her,* *and it happens,*
that she find no favor in his eyes, *because he hath found some uncleanness in her,*	*if she does not find favor in his eyes,* *because he has found some uncleanness in her,*
then let him write her a bill of divorcement, *and give it in her hand,* *and send her out of his house.*	*and he writes her a certificate of divorce,* *and gives it in her hand,* *and sends her out of his house,*
Second Law, 24:2	
And when she is departed out of his house,	*and she departs out of his house,*
she may go and be another man's wife.	*and goes and becomes another man's wife,*
Third Law, 24:3-4a	
And if the latter husband hate her, *and write her a bill of divorcement,* *and giveth it in her hand,* *and sendeth her out of his house,*	*and the latter husband hates her,* *and writes her a certificate of divorce,* *and gives it in her hand,* *and sends her out of his house,*
or if the latter husband die, which took her to be his wife,	*or if the latter husband dies, who took her to be his wife,*
her former husband, which sent her away, may not take her again to be his wife, after that she is defiled.	*then her former husband, which sent her away, may not take her again to be his wife, after she is defiled.*
The Explanation, 24:4b	
For that is abomination before the Lord, and thou shalt not cause the land to sin, which the Lord thy God giveth thee for an inheritance.	*For that is an abomination before the Lord, and you shall not cause the land to sin, the land that the Lord your God gives you for an inheritance.*

1. The one-law interpretation is the **more natural translation** of the Hebrew text.
2. The three-law interpretation leads to **contradictions**
among the three laws.
3. The **explanation** "*For that is abomination before the Lord
...*" (verse 4) fits the one-law interpretation.
4. **Jeremiah** cites the passage in a way that presumes the
one-law interpretation.

The Grammar of Deuteronomy 24:1-4

The simplest reading of Deuteronomy 24:1-4 is as one law
rather than three. In Hebrew, there is no repeated "if" at the beginning of 24:2 or 24:3 (the start of the supposed second and
third laws), and the only distinctive Hebrew construction that
would indicate a "then" comes at the beginning of 24:4. (This
construction is a disjunctive clause, that is, one that begins with
something other than a verb. I've marked it with the word "*then*"
in the right-hand column. A disjunctive clause also appears in
the middle of verse 3, "*or if the latter husband dies,*" but nobody
confuses this clause for a conclusion.) There is nothing in the
text to suggest that there are three laws. If we follow only the
evidence that the text gives us, we will read 24:1-3 as one long
"if" and 24:4a as the "then."

Three Paradoxical Laws

Not only is the one-law interpretation simpler linguistically,
it also avoids certain contradictions that arise among the three
laws of the three-law interpretation.

The three laws of the three-law interpretation are:

1. A man may divorce his wife, thus ending their marriage
(24:1).
2. A divorced woman may marry someone else (24:2).
3. If anything happens to the second marriage, the woman
may not return to the first husband, because she is defiled
(24:3, 4).

The first law, allowing divorce, leads logically to the second law, allowing marriage to someone else. If the first marriage is really gone, there can be no objection to remarriage. The first law and the third, though, are in conflict, as are the second and the third. Let's look at these conflicts.

A Divorce That Doesn't Work.—The first law conflicts with the third law, forbidding reconciliation of the first couple. If the first marriage is really gone, no relationship remains between the woman and her first husband. If the second husband dies, they should be able to marry one another as well as anybody else. Under the three-law interpretation, they may marry other people, but not one another. Some sort of relation remains between the woman and her first husband, in spite of the divorce of Deuteronomy 24:1.

A Marriage That Defiles.—The second and third laws also conflict. The second law permits the woman to remarry, but the third law says that she is "*defiled*" as a result of remarrying.

Leviticus 18 uses the word "*defiled*" to describe sexual sin.

> *You shall not lie carnally with your neighbor's wife, to **defile** yourself with her* (Lev 18:20).

> *Do not **defile yourselves** in any of these things, for in all these things the nations are **defiled**, the nations that I cast out from before you* (Lev 18:24).

> *You shall keep my ordinance, so that you do not commit any of the abominable customs that were committed before you, and so that you do not **defile yourselves** in them* (Lev 18:30).

The third law says that the woman is "*defiled*" by the second marriage, and so views its consummation as sexual sin. Yet the second law allows her to remarry. Thus the second law and the third law, like the first law and the third law, are contradictory.

If there are three laws in Deuteronomy 24:1-4, they contradict one another. The one-law interpretation has no such problem. It sanctions neither divorce nor remarriage, but only tells what to do in one particular combination of these events.

How Does Moses Explain the Law?

Both interpretations agree that Deuteronomy 24:1-4 forbids the reconciliation of a divorced couple if the wife has married someone else after the divorce. After giving the law, Moses explains this prohibition.

> *For that is an abomination before the Lord, and you shall not cause the land to sin, the land that the Lord your God gives you for an inheritance* (Deut 24:4b).

This explanation helps us choose between the interpretations.

Under the three-law interpretation, the explanation is confusing. If divorce really does dissolve a marriage, why should a later reconciliation be *"an abomination before the Lord"*? In the three-law interpretation, both the first and the second marriage are gone. They should not have any effect on remarriage.

The explanation does fit the one-law interpretation. Divorce is not God's way to dissolve a marriage, but only a human attempt to do so. People cannot completely untie the knot that God has tied. A special relationship remains between man and wife. This persistent relationship makes reconciliation after a second marriage abominable.

Deuteronomy 24:4 is the only verse in the Bible that uses the verb *"to sin"* to describe *"the land."* Jeremiah uses a synonym when he paraphrases this law: *"Shall not that land be greatly polluted?"* (Jer 3:1). Among other passages, Numbers 35:31-33 talks about the pollution of the land. Though the specific causes of pollution differ in Numbers and in Deuteronomy, both talk about averting pollution. How can Numbers can help us understand Deuteronomy?

Murder Also "Pollutes the Land" — In Numbers 35, God tells the nation Israel how to judge and punish the crime of murder. The conclusion of this chapter talks about polluting the land.

> *You shall take no atonement for the life of a murderer who is guilty of death, but he shall surely be put to*

*death. … So you shall not **pollute** the land where you
are, for blood **pollutes** the land, and no atonement can
be made for the land, for the blood that is shed on it, except by the blood of him who shed it* (Num 35:31,33).

Bloodshed by murder "*pollutes the land*." The damage can
be reversed, by punishing the murderer. Otherwise, the pollution
remains.

Ever since the time of Noah, the penalty for murder is death.
God tells Noah,

*Whoever sheds man's blood, by man shall his blood be
shed* (Gen 9:6).

Under Moses, the responsibility for this judgment falls on the
relatives of the dead man. One of them, called "*the avenger of
blood*" in Numbers 35, seeks out the killer to slay him. The killer
flees to a "city of refuge" for protection until the elders of his
home city extradite him for trial (Deut 19:12). If the trial finds
that the killing was accidental, he returns to the city of refuge,
safe from the avenger of blood. But if he is guilty, he is delivered
to the avenger of blood for execution.

The law of murder makes the avenger of blood responsible
for preventing pollution of the land. The avenger of blood ful-
fills this duty by executing the murderer. The avenger of blood
is not allowed to forgive and release the murderer. More is at
stake than a personal vendetta between the murderer and the victim's family. God's law has been broken, and it is God's judgment, not personal vengeance, that the avenger must execute.
Whatever the avenger's personal feelings toward the murderer,
he has a duty as the agent of God's judgment.

How Is Adultery Like Murder? — Adultery, as well as
murder, "pollutes the land":

*She polluted the land and committed adultery with
stone and tree* (Jer 3:9).

Under the one-law interpretation of Deuteronomy 24, divorce
and remarriage is really adultery, for the divorce has no divine

sanction. In spite of the "*certificate of divorce*" that the first husband gives the woman in Deuteronomy 24:1, she is still his wife.
When she marries the second man, she commits adultery against
the first, and threatens the land with pollution.

Numbers 35 shows that the pollution that sin brings on the
land can be removed if the sin is judged. In the case of murder,
the prosecutor is the avenger of blood. There is also a prosecutor for the sin of adultery. It is the first husband. Throughout
the Law of Moses, he is the one who must bring charges against
an adulterous wife. In Deuteronomy 22:13-21, he accuses her of
premarital impurity. In Numbers 5:11-31, he accuses her of unfaithfulness after marriage. The analogy of Numbers 35 suggests
that in both cases he is not only defending his own honor, but
also enforcing God's law.

As with murder, the judgment on adultery must not be by-
passed, or the land will remain polluted. It is not just a question
of the relationship between the man and his wife, but of the dis-
charge of God's law among his subjects. Of course, it is unlikely
that the first husband will accuse his wife of adultery through
remarriage if he has first divorced her. It is even less likely that
any society that recognizes the divorce will accept the charges.
Still, before God, the husband is responsible to prosecute his
wife's sin. If he drops the charges, the land remains defiled, for
he has abandoned his responsibility to execute God's justice.

Now the reasoning behind the law of reconciliation is clear.
A husband may take back his divorced wife if she has not remarried, for the divorce does not change their union in God's eyes.
However, if she marries someone else, she commits adultery
against her first husband. Now he is responsible before God to
prosecute her sin. If he accepts her back, he effectively pardons
the sin. Yet he has no authority to pardon her, for it is God's law,
not his, that demands satisfaction. By refusing to satisfy that law,
he leaves the land polluted with adultery.

This explanation does not work under the three-law interpretation. If the first law authorizes divorce and the second author-

izes remarriage, the third can hardly hold the original husband responsible for carrying out God's judgment on what God has authorized. The one-law interpretation does not authorize either the divorce or the first remarriage. It simply forbids the first husband from being reconciled to his wife, because he is now responsible for judging her and thus removing the pollution caused by her adultery.

How Does Jeremiah Use This Law?

The prophet Jeremiah understands Deuteronomy 24:1-4 to contain only one law, not three. He cites the passage when he condemns Judah for idolatry, a condition he describes as spiritual adultery. He writes,

> *"They say, 'If a man sends out his wife, and she goes from him and becomes another man's, may he return to her again? Would not that land be greatly polluted?' In your case, you have played the harlot with many lovers, and would you now return to me?" says the Lord* (Jer 3:1).

Jeremiah argues that if the law forbids reunion with one's spouse after adultery with even a single partner, Judah can hardly expect the Lord to welcome her back after she has been unfaithful with many lovers. He paraphrases the law as a single long condition, followed by a conclusion, probably to be understood as a question, *"May he return to her again?"* This question clearly expects a negative answer. Under the conditions described, restoration is impossible. Jeremiah reads the law, not as three separate instructions, but as a single law. In our terms, he follows the one-law interpretation.

One Law or Three?

We have found four reasons to prefer the one-law interpretation of Deuteronomy 24:1-4. The one-law interpretation is more natural grammatically, it avoids contradictions to which the other interpretation leads, it explains why reconciliation is *"abom-*

ination before the Lord," and it is consistent with Jeremiah's paraphrase.

THE INTERPRETATION OF DEUTERONOMY 24:1-4 IN THE FIRST CENTURY

One of the great theological debates in first century Judaism presumes the three-law interpretation of Deuteronomy 24:1-4. The protagonists are the noted rabbis Hillel and Shammai. Both were born before the birth of the Lord.

These two rabbis both follow the three-law interpretation, and allow divorce in the case of "*some uncleanness.*" They differ over what sort of "*uncleanness*" would justify divorce. Hillel teaches that an offense as slight as burning the supper would justify divorce, while Shammai holds that the law refers to a major issue of impurity (Babylonian Talmud, *Gittin* 90a).

Shammai's position is unnecessary in a society that obeys Deuteronomy 22:13-29, because a woman who exhibits "*some uncleanness*" in the strict sense would be put to death, as summarized in Table 3 (page 21), and the question of divorce would not arise. On pages 27-28, we saw evidence that Jews in the first century are moving away from the death penalty for impurity. The agreement of Hillel and Shammai on the three-law interpretation, and the attention they give to the conditions for divorce, reinforce that evidence. As the nation abandons the biblical provision of Deuteronomy 22:13-29 for dealing with immorality, it seeks other ways to end unacceptable marriages. Under these circumstances, it is not surprising that people would prefer a grammatically and contextually awkward reading of Deuteronomy 24 that allows a loophole for divorce.

First-century Judaism thus departs in two ways from Moses' law concerning marriage. The leaders hesitate to impose the teaching of Deuteronomy 22:13-29 that impurity should lead to capital punishment, and they strain the interpretation of Deuteronomy 24:1-4 to create a permission for divorce in the case of *"some uncleanness."*

In the next chapter, we will bring these ideas together to understand the Lord's teaching. If you have read this far without looking ahead to my solution, you may want to pause and see if you can assemble the clues yourself. In summary, they are:

–   The Lord forbids a man to dismiss his wife *"except for fornication."*

–   In case of dismissal, the man is allowed to remarry, but any attempt to determine the state of the woman and a future husband leads to contradictions.

–   In each of the Lord's teachings on divorce, he exhorts the Jewish teachers to return to the Law of Moses.

–   If a wife is found guilty of fornication, the law of Moses does not authorize divorce, but commands that she be put to death.

Keeping all these clues in mind, can you see what the Lord means when he authorizes a man to dismiss his wife for fornication?

4

OUR LORD CORRECTS JEWISH ERRORS

The context of Matthew 5:31-32 requires us to understand the Lord's words in a way that corrects Jewish misunderstanding of the law. The last two chapters discussed two such misunderstandings: the neglect of the death penalty specified in Deuteronomy 22:13-29 for impurity, and the reanalysis of Deuteronomy 24:1-4 as three laws rather than one to provide a legal justification for divorce. The Lord challenges both of these errors.

- Both Matthew 5:32 and 19:9 challenge the Jewish error about **Deuteronomy 24:1-4**.
- The vocabulary used by the Jewish leaders shows their **careless handling** of the Old Testament law.
- The Lord uses their vocabulary to challenge the Jewish error about **Deuteronomy 22:13-29**.
- Our Lord's teaching presumes a civil society that operates according to the Mosaic law. We consider its relevance for us today, in western society.

CHALLENGING THE UNDERSTANDING OF DEUTERONOMY 24:1-4

Chapter 3 distinguished between the three-law interpretation of Deuteronomy 24:1-4, which authorizes divorce, and the one-law interpretation, which recognizes that divorce takes place but denies that it ends a marriage. This distinction lies at the root of the Lord's challenge to the Pharisees in both Matthew 5:31-32 and Matthew 19:3-9.

In Matthew 5:31, the Lord quotes the Pharisees' understanding of Deuteronomy 24:1-4.

> *Furthermore it has been said,*
>   *"Whoever dismisses his wife, let him give her*
>   *a divorce."*

The phrase *"Let him give her a divorce"* is the Pharisees' paraphrase of Deuteronomy 24:1, *"he writes her a certificate of divorce."* *"Let him give"* is a form of command. (The English imperative "let us give" is a command to someone **to** whom we are speaking. English does not have a special verb form to give a command to someone **about** whom we are speaking. Biblical Greek has distinctive imperative forms for both situations, a second person imperative to command the person to whom we are speaking and a third person imperative, which the Pharisees use, to command the person about whom we are speaking.) They are saying, "If you want to dismiss your wife, here is the way you should do it: give her a divorce." The LXX of Deuteronomy 24:1 does not use the imperative at this point, but simply the indicative, as does the Hebrew. Paraphrasing the verb as an imperative, *"Let him give,"* accepts the three-law interpretation. This is the position that the Lord attributes to those whom he is criticizing, and that he counters in verse 32, when he says, *"But I say unto you."*

The interchange in Perea (Mark 10:2-4; Matthew 19:7-8) confirms this difference between the Pharisees and the Lord. Matthew and Mark record different portions of the conversation. One key to understanding the discussion is to observe the repeated contrast between what Moses *commands* and what he *allows*.

In Mark 10:2-4, the Pharisees introduce the contrast:

> *The Pharisees … asked him, "Is it lawful for a man to dismiss his wife?", tempting him.*
> *And he, answering, said unto them, "What did Moses **command** you?"*

*And they said, "Moses **allowed** to write a certificate of
divorce, and to dismiss."*

The Pharisees ask whether divorce is lawful. They do not expect the Lord to say "Yes," because they think he holds the same
view that John did. If the Lord says "No," they will report him
to Herod. The Lord detects their malice, and answers by asking
them what Moses commands.

Like most Jews of their day, the Pharisees believe that Moses
not only allowed, but in fact approved, divorce. However, they
hesitate to press this point, since they wish to lead the Lord into a clear condemnation of divorce. To elicit the Lord's view,
they must make the law seem ambiguous and invite his interpretation. So they respond, *"Moses **allowed** to write a certificate of divorce."*

Since they invite an interpretation, the Lord gives them one.

*Jesus, answering, said unto them, "Because of your
hardness of heart he wrote you this precept"* (Mark
10:5).

Moses knew that the people had hard hearts, and that they
would stumble into divorce. He wrote Deuteronomy 24:1-4 to
tell people what to do when they find themselves in such a cir-
cumstance. But God never intended that man and wife should
separate. Christ reminds the Pharisees that Moses not only wrote
Deuteronomy 24:1-4 but also recorded the institution of marriage in Genesis:

*But from the beginning of creation God made them
male and female. Because of this a man shall leave his
father and mother, and be joined to his wife, and the
two shall become one flesh. So then they are no more
two, but one flesh. What therefore God has joined together, let not man separate* (Mark 10:6-9).

The Pharisees want the Lord to comment on Deuteronomy
24:1-4 and divorce. The Lord deflects their attention to Genesis 3 and marriage. (The Lord is not quoting Genesis to revoke

Deuteronomy 24:1-4, but to correct the Pharisees' erroneous interpretation of Deuteronomy 24:1 as authorizing divorce.) Frustrated, they try to pull him back to Deuteronomy. This time, they show their real attitude toward the passage by calling it a *"command."* Matthew records this part of the conversation.

> *[The Pharisees] say unto him, "Why did Moses then **command** to give a certificate of divorce, and to dismiss her?" He says unto them, "Moses because of your hardness of heart **allowed** you to dismiss your wives, but from the beginning it was not so"* (Matt 19:7, 8).

The Lord answers, not by opposing Moses, but by opposing their interpretation. They claim, "Moses commanded." He responds, "Moses allowed." Moses' legislation does not command divorce. It only makes allowance for it, by telling people what to do if they are divorced.

The Pharisees see divorce as a right guaranteed by the Law, following the three-law interpretation of Deuteronomy 24:1-4. The Lord says that it merely makes provision for sin. Like Jeremiah, he interprets the entire paragraph as a single command.

JEWISH ABUSE OF VOCABULARY

The Pharisees' teaching cited in Matthew 5:31 is not only an erroneous interpretation of Deuteronomy 24:1, but also a loose paraphrase rather than a quotation of that verse. The Lord focuses on one detail of their paraphrase to highlight their underlying error.

The Pharisees' paraphrase of Deuteronomy 24:1 in Matthew 5:31 deviates from the original in four ways.

1. Moses uses an indicative verb, describing the fact of divorce. Even the LXX faithfully reproduces this detail, but the Pharisees' paraphrase, reflecting the three-law interpretation, replaces it with an imperative.

2. Moses writes of a *"certificate of divorce."* They ignore the *"certificate"* and speak only of *divorce.* (In Matthew 19:7, they do use the entire phrase.)

3. Having dropped the *"certificate,"* they do not speak of *"writ[ing],"* as does Moses, but only of *"giv[ing] a divorce."*

4. Moses uses specific language to describe the separation of man and wife. The Pharisees do not use his terms, but introduce a different verb, *"dismiss."*

The fourth deviation is the least obvious to us, since most English versions do not maintain the distinction between Moses' language and the Pharisees' word *"dismiss."* This distinction is critical in understanding the Lord's response. He develops a word play with the Pharisees' term, a word play that would be impossible if they used Moses' language.

What would it mean for the Pharisees to use Moses' language? We are studying a record, written in Greek, of a sermon that may have been delivered in Aramaic, concerning a Hebrew law. The Old Testament was written in Hebrew and Aramaic, not Greek, so strictly speaking no Old Testament word occurs in the New Testament. However, the Jews of the first century A.D. used the LXX, a Greek translation of the Hebrew Old Testament, just as we use English translations of the Hebrew and Greek Bible. The LXX shows the commonly accepted Greek equivalents for the Hebrew words for divorce. (Appendix 1 discusses this principle in more detail.)

In Deuteronomy 24:1-4, Moses uses three Hebrew expressions to describe the separation of man and wife. Whenever the Old Testament describes divorce, it always uses one or another of these expressions. The English translations of these expressions are *"certificate of divorce"* (Hebrew *sēper kərîtut,* Greek *biblion apostasion), "send her out"* (Hebrew *šlḥ Piel,* variously translated in the LXX as *apostellō* and *exapostellō* [Deut. 24], elsewhere often translated *"put her away"*), and *"she is departed"* (Hebrew *yṣʾ Qal* (Deut 24:2), *Hifil* (Ezra 10:3, 19), Greek *erchomai, aperchomai, ekballō, ekferō).*

When the Pharisees describe divorce, they do not use any of the Greek equivalents of these Hebrew expressions. Instead, they introduce a new word *(apoluō),* one that the LXX never uses for divorce. This verb, which I translate *"dismiss,"* is a common word for divorce in Greek of the first century A.D., but it is never used in the LXX to speak of marital separation.

In itself, using a secular word for divorce rather than a biblical word is not wrong. When Paul discusses divorce in 1 Corinthians 7, he uses words *(afiēmi, chorizō)* that the Old Testament does not use to describe divorce. But the Pharisees are not just discussing divorce. They are citing Deuteronomy 24:1. Because they substitute a new word in an old passage, that word attracts the Lord's attention. "So you Pharisees want to talk about *"dismissing* a wife?" he might say. "Then let me tell you what the Law says about *dismissing.*" Once we realize that he is playing with their new word, we can understand his answer in a new way.

CHALLENGING THE NEGLECT OF DEUTERONOMY 22

The Jewish error in explaining the structure of Deuteronomy 24:1-4 was motivated by their neglect of the biblical penalty for fornication in Deuteronomy 22:13-29. The proper way to end a marriage for impurity is by stoning the guilty spouse, which leaves the innocent member free to remarry. Our Lord's words in both Matthew 5:32 and 19:9 indicate that fornication allows remarriage. It looks as though the fornication clause is reminding the Jews of the biblical way to deal with fornication: not by divorce, but by the death penalty.

One might object that Matthew 5:32 and 19:9 do not mention death, but only putting away. Let's look more closely. In both verses, the Lord adopts the Pharisee's word for divorce, *"dismiss."* This verb never means "divorce" in the Greek Old Testament, but it does have two meanings of interest to us.

The literal meaning of the Pharisees' word is "dismiss." This meaning appears, for example, in the title to Psalm 34 (Ps. 33:1 in the LXX):

A Psalm of David, when he changed his face before
*Abimelech, and he **dismissed** him, and he departed.*

The title alludes to the episode in 1 Samuel 21:10-22:1. David, fleeing from Saul, seeks refuge with Achish, king of the Philistines. (The word "Abimelech" in the title of the Psalm is not a name, but a title, just as "Pharaoh" is the title of the kings of Egypt.) The men of Achish recognize David as an enemy. To escape, David pretends that he is insane, and Achish, in disgust, sends him away. The title to the psalm describes this sending away with *"dismissed."*

It is easy to see how the Greek word for *"dismiss"* comes to describe divorce, where a man sends a woman away from his household. The word develops this meaning by New Testament times. It appears in this sense in Dionys. Hal. 2, 25, 7 (who lived in the last 60 years before Christ) and Diodorus Siculus 12, 18, 1 (also dating to the first century B.C.). But the Greek Old Testament never uses it in this sense. (In the apocrypha, 1 Esdras 9:36 uses the verb to describe Ezra's separation of mixed unions. It describes separation from children as well as wives, so it should be understood as "send away" rather than "divorce." The longer book shows that these separations were annulments, not divorce.)

The other Old Testament meaning of *"dismiss"* of interest to us appears in Genesis 15:2. Because we are interested in the usage of the Greek word, our translation follows the LXX, which differs slightly from the Hebrew.

And Abram said, "Lord God, what will you give me?
*For I am **dismissed** childless, and the son of Masek of*
those born in my house is this Eliezer of Damascus."

Abram is saying, "I am going to die without any children, and according to custom, one of the children of my slaves will be my heir." The text uses the verb *"dismissed"* as a euphemism for death.

Another example is Numbers 20:28-29 (again following the LXX),

And Aaron died upon the top of the mount. ... And all
*the congregation saw that Aaron was **dismissed** , and*
all the house of Israel mourned Aaron thirty days.

God tells Moses and Aaron that Aaron's time has come to die. They ascend Mount Hor, where Aaron expires. Again, *"dismissed"* describes death.

So the verb *"dismiss"* can mean "dismiss from life." It is used this way in the New Testament. Luke's Gospel records how the aged Simeon greets the infant Jesus in the temple. God promised Simeon that he would not die until he saw the Messiah, and now the promise is fulfilled. So Simeon prays,

*Now **dismiss** your servant, Lord, according to your*
word, in peace. For my eyes have seen your salvation
(Luke 2:29-30).

Simeon knows that his time has come. With the words *"Dismiss your servant,"* he invites the Lord to take him.

This usage of the word is attested in nonbiblical Greek writers as well.

In Sophocles' play *Antigone*, written in the fifth century B.C., King Creon laments over his dead son,

Alas, alas.
You have died; *you have been dismissed* (*apoluō* aor-
ist passive indicative),
By my folly, not your own (1267-1269).

A few lines later, Creon learns that his queen has also died, and asks for details using the same word,

How then *was she dismissed?* (*apoluō* aorist
middle) (1314)

The other classical examples of this usage come from the fourth century B.C., and all involve a noun, "departure" *(apolus-is),* that is a close derivative of the verb that we are studying.

– Diogenes Laertius, in his biography of the philosopher

Lyco, includes a copy of this philosopher's will. Lyco stipulates that, "after my *departure*," one of his brothers should dispose of oil from his olive trees in a certain way (5.71). The noun is here used in a legal document to specify decease.

– The naturalist Theophrastus describes a poison that "produces an easy and painless *departure*" (*Enquiry into Plants*, 9.16.8).
– Aristotle claims that "death in old age is painless. … The *departure* of the soul happens utterly without sensation" (*On Respiration*, 479a.22).

We now know two important facts about the verb "dismiss" that the Pharisees have introduced into the discussion, and that our Lord picks up in his comments.

1. It is never used in the Old Testament to describe marital separation. Thus it attracts the Lord's attention when the Pharisees use it to paraphrase the Mosaic Law on divorce.
2. In both Testaments, it can mean "dismiss from life."

If we keep these two meanings in mind as we read Matthew 5:32, the puzzle about fornication becomes much clearer.

Whoever dismisses his wife, except for the cause of fornication, causes her to commit adultery.

There are two ways that a man may *"dismiss"* his wife. He may divorce her, putting her out of his house. In this case he causes her to commit adultery, for she will be without support unless she remarries. But if she is guilty of fornication, he has another option. He can dismiss her from life by having her tried and stoned. In this case he does not cause her to commit adultery, for she is dead and so cannot remarry. In addition, her death means that he is now free to remarry. This harsh verdict shows how terrible fornication is in the eyes of the Lord.

Deuteronomy 22:13-29 prescribes stoning not only for adultery (unfaithfulness after betrothal or marriage), but also for uncleanness before marriage that is concealed from the bridegroom.

The word *"fornication"* covers both of these cases, and so the Lord uses it in Matthew 5:32 and 19:9.

The second half of these verses is also clear.

> *And whoever marries a dismissed woman commits
> adultery.*

Remarriage is possible only when the woman is *"dismissed"* in such a way as to leave her alive. Whenever the woman survives her dismissal, remarriage is adultery, both for her and for her new spouse. When a woman is dismissed by stoning because of fornication, the question of remarriage does not arise.

So the Lord rejects the Pharisees' notion that God sanctions divorce. Remarriage after divorce is adultery. By introducing the case of fornication, with its associated penalty of stoning, he emphasizes that only death can break the marriage bond. His answer reflects not only the Old Testament notion that "the Lord hates divorce" (Mal 2:16), but also the law condemning impure wives to death (Deut 22:13-29).

This background lets us understand the Lord's words as a play on the word "dismiss." We may paraphrase his argument:

> Your teachers tell you that you may *"dismiss"* your wives by means of a certificate of divorce. They are adopting pagan language instead of biblical language to describe the separation. Their word means more than they intend. If you *"dismiss"* your spouse, then remarriage is adulterous for both her and you. There is only one exception. The law does allow you to *"dismiss"* a spouse for fornication, by putting her to death. In this case, you are free to remarry, since all will agree that death breaks the marriage bond.

This interpretation solves all of the dilemmas associated with conventional readings of the fornication clause.

- The logical inconsistencies within 5:32 and 19:9 vanish if dismissal for fornication consists of the death of the guilty party.
- The fornication clause no longer agrees with Shammai's position, but is a radical departure from the growing Jewish consensus in favor of divorce. Thus it is consistent with the pervasive criticism of the Pharisees' interpretations throughout Matthew 5.
- Matthew is no longer in conflict with Mark and Luke. Each Gospel has a different audience. Matthew writes for Jewish readers, who should know the Mosaic law and thus understand the reference to *"dismiss[ing] for fornication."* Without this background, the Gentile readers addressed by Mark and Luke would not catch the allusion to the death penalty. They would misunderstand the clause to authorize a form of divorce that leaves both members free to remarry, which is the direct opposite of what the Lord intends. Ironically, most modern Christians, missing the Old Testament allusion, make the very error that Mark and Luke, in omitting the clause, seek to avoid.

APPLYING THE LORD'S WORDS TODAY

When our Lord speaks of *"dismiss[ing] for fornication,"* he has in mind the death penalty specified in Deuteronomy 22:13-29 for impurity that would interfere with a marriage. This understanding is intellectually satisfying, because it solves the puzzles that the Gospel accounts otherwise present. It is also morally satisfying, because it sets the offended spouse free to remarry. But in modern western society, which does not enforce the death penalty for fornication, it is frustrating. What option does it leave to a believer married to an unfaithful spouse? Since a modern divorce does not end the marriage in God's eyes, a divorced believer whose spouse has remarried is condemned to remain without a partner as long as the spouse lives.

Let's be very clear that capital punishment can only be applied by a civil magistrate (Rom 13:4), not the individual believer (Matt 5:39). Israel, as a civil institution, had the divine authority to wield the sword. An individual believer does not, and our Lord's words do not authorize individuals to do away with errant spouses.

Though our society does not enforce this law, God is still the one who sovereignly *"kills and makes alive"* (1 Sam 2:6). A believer who is divorced by an unfaithful spouse must live in celibacy as long as the spouse is alive. But God can at any moment remove the unfaithful spouse through death and free his child to remarry. In Israel, God gave that power to the magistrate. If our magistrates do not enforce this law, God can still exercise that power independently of the magistrate and set his child free, in his time.

5

PAUL'S TEACHING ON DIVORCE

The Lord Jesus uttered only eleven verses on the subject of divorce and remarriage, mostly restating the same two principles: divorce is wrong, and remarriage after divorce is adultery.

The most extensive discussion of marriage in the New Testament, 1 Corinthians 7, extends over 40 verses. The longer book discusses this chapter in detail. We consider it briefly because its teachings are sometimes understood as superseding the Lord's teaching by allowing divorce and remarriage.

– We begin by explaining some **puzzles** in 1 Corinthians 7.
– This explanation shows that, far from contradicting our Lord, Paul **quotes him** as the basis for his teaching.
– In the light of this agreement, we **examine the texts** that have been understood to allow divorce and remarriage.
– We consider the **implications** of Paul's endorsement of our Lord's teaching for our situation today.

A CHAPTER FOR LOVERS

Many people think of Paul as a crotchety old bachelor who views romantic love as a snare of the devil. If you ask for evidence, they turn to 1 Corinthians 7 and point out such gems as "*It is good for a man not to touch a woman*" (verse 1), "*He who causes her to marry does well, but he who does not cause her to marry does better*" (verse 38), and "*She is happier if she abides [unmarried]*" (verse 40).

This impression is superficial, as we can see by examining some puzzles to which it leads and reconstructing the correspondence behind this chapter.

Some Puzzles in 1 Corinthians 7

If 1 Corinthians 7 opposes marriage, it contradicts both itself and other writings by Paul.

Puzzles Within — Paul begins, *"It is good for a man not to touch a woman"* (1 Cor 7:1b). If these words advocate the single life, the next sentence is very strange.

> *Nevertheless, because of fornication, let every man have his own wife, and let every woman have her own husband* (1 Cor 7:2).

Instead of building on the theme of celibacy, he immediately says that everybody should be married. Verses 3 through 5 show that he is not talking about platonic unions.

The internal puzzle lies in the tension between verses 1 and 2. If Paul wants Christians to stay single, why does he write verse 2? If he wants them to marry, why does he write verse 1?

Puzzles Without — If Paul is against marriage in 1 Corinthians, he changes his view in later Epistles.

– He condemns false teachers who *"forbid to marry"* (1 Tim 4:3).
– He advises *"younger women to marry, bear children, guide the house"* (1 Tim 5:14).
– He even uses marriage as a picture of Christ's union with his church (Eph 5).

Perhaps he changed his mind! Then again, perhaps the traditional interpretation of 1 Corinthians 7 is incorrect.

Reconstructing a Lost Letter

Paul's words are only half of a conversation. Paul begins the chapter, *"Now concerning the things of which you wrote to me."* He is responding to a letter from the Corinthians. What sort of letter from them could lead to the contrasting statements with which Paul begins his response?

Perhaps the Corinthians wrote something like this to Paul:

> Dear Paul,
>
> You're going to be so proud of us! The Lord has led us to new heights of devotion and spirituality. We are the bride of Christ, and we have resolved to belong to no one but him. All the single folks in the church reject the prospect of marriage. Isn't that great? Marriage is just a concession to the flesh, and we are above such temptations.
>
> The married Christians are a bit sad that they didn't see these truths earlier, before they succumbed to the carnal lure of matrimony. To avoid sinning in the future, they have all agreed not to touch their spouses. From now on we are brothers and sisters in Christ, with no thought of unholy desire to cloud our Christian love.
>
> In Christ,
> Your Friends at Corinth

How would Paul respond?

He cannot endorse such a scheme. This teaching is just the sort of heresy against which he writes in 1 Timothy 4:3. But the Corinthians are not heretics. They sincerely want to serve the Lord. Paul must correct their ideas gently, or he may alienate them.

Sometimes friends approach us with a very bad idea that they think is very good. We may respond, "That's a nice idea. But have you considered … ?" We first try to find something good in what they say, something with which we can agree. Then we present the facts as we see them.

Paul uses this strategy in 1 Corinthians 7. His opening words are a summary of the Corinthians' position: *"It is good for a man not to touch a woman."* There is something noble and exalted about the idea of Christians devoting themselves wholly to the service of God. In practice, though, this idea will not work, as he explains in verse 2. Celibacy does not quench physical appetites. It only removes the legitimate channel for their expression. In theory, undivided devotion to God *looks* better than the distraction of marriage. In fact, marriage *is* better than the sin of fornication.

As a response to the Corinthians' letter, Paul's apparently negative comments about marriage in this chapter reflect, not a strong personal distaste for marriage, but his tact in dealing with his friends. Far from condemning marriage, in most cases he recommends it.

THE WORDS OF OUR LORD JESUS CHRIST

In 1 Timothy 6:3-4, Paul criticizes anyone who does not *"consent to ... the words of our Lord Jesus Christ."* Paul's writings show that he knows many of the Lord's earthly teachings, even though, at the time he wrote, the Gospels probably were not yet written down in the form that we have them now. 1 Corinthians 7 contains two examples of references to the Lord's teaching, one in verses 7 and 17, and the other in verses 10-11.

The Gift from God (1 Cor 7:7, 17)

The positions we have just reconstructed for Paul and the Corinthians are very similar to the positions of our Lord and his disciples in Matthew 19. As Table 5 shows, both the disciples in Matthew 19 and the Corinthians suggest celibacy as a general policy, and both the Lord and Paul caution their hearers not to go beyond their individual gifts.

In Matthew 19, the disciples react to the Lord's teaching about divorce with the words,

Table 5: Parallels between
Matthew 19 and 1 Corinthians 7

Students: Let's all stay single	Disciples (Matt 19:10)	Corinthians (Lost letter)
Teacher: Be sure of your gift	Lord Jesus (Matt 19:11)	Paul (1 Cor 7:7, 17)

If the case of the man be so with the wife, it is not expedient to marry (Matt 19:10).

Like the Corinthians, they advocate celibacy. The Lord responds,

Not all receive this word, but those to whom it is given (Matt 19:11).

Only God can enable the single life.

Paul, facing the same misunderstanding on the part of his students, says the same thing.

Every one has his own gift from God. (1 Cor 7:7)
As God has distributed to every one, … so let him walk (1 Cor 7:17).

Given Paul's commitment to build on the Lord's words and the similarity between his teaching and Matt 19:11, it seems likely that he is alluding to the Lord's teaching.

The Separation Paragraph (1 Cor 7:10-11)

1 Corinthians 7:10-11 contain a second, even clearer, reference to the Lord's teaching. He divides the church at Corinth into three groups: the "unmarried and widows" (7:8-9), the "married" (7:10-11), and the "rest" (7:12-16). The verses about the "rest" describe believers' spouses as unbelieving, so the "married" must be believers married to other believers.

Paul first addresses believing couples.

To the married I command, yet not I, but the Lord, "Let not the wife depart from her husband. But if she should depart, let her remain unmarried, or be reconciled to

*her husband. And let not the husband put away his
wife"* (1 Cor 7:10-11).

(The word "unmarried" refers only to her civil state, for if she
were unmarried in God's eyes, there could be no objection to her
remarriage. See the longer book for further discussion.)

Paul traces his instruction to the Lord's teaching in the Gospels, which is in turn an exposition of the Law of Moses. The
Law allows marriages only between two Israelites, and the
Lord's words also assume a Jewish context, in which both part-
ners claim to be under the old covenant. So they are a good basis
for Paul's teaching to couples where both members profess salvation under the new covenant.

Paul adds nothing new to what we have already seen in the
Gospels. Neither the husband nor the wife should initiate a separation. If they do separate, they are not free to remarry, except
to one another.

When Paul turns to marriages between believers and unbelievers (verses 12-16), he contemplates a relation that does not
exist in the Old Testament. It's not just that the Law of Moses
disapproves of mixed marriages. Because Israel is a civil government as well as a spiritual institution, it defines what is re-
cognized as marriage among its members. Based on Ezra 9-10,
the longer book concludes that a union between an Israelite and
a pagan was invalid under the old covenant. In modern terms,
you couldn't get a marriage license for such a wedding. The
godly response to such unions was to annul them.

Paul teaches that the standards have changed under the new
covenant.

*If any brother has an unbelieving wife, ... let him not
put her away.
And any woman who has an unbelieving husband, ...
let her not put him away* (1 Cor 7:12, 13).

The church is a spiritual organism, not a civil government
with authority to define what constitutes a marriage. Believers

with unbelieving spouses are not to follow Ezra's instructions to separate. The Lord's discussions with the Pharisees did not directly address this case, so Paul acknowledges that this revelation is new through him.

But to the rest speak I, not the Lord (1 Cor 7:12).

His words are no less inspired than those uttered by Lord during his earthly ministry. Paul is commenting on the channel of revelation, not its authority.

The distinction between verses 10 and 12 show that Paul knows of the Lord's teaching, and concurs with it. As a careful student of the Scriptures, he distinguishes mixed marriages from those between professing believers. Even so, his main conclusion in the mixed case conforms to the Lord's instruction: the believer (the only member of the union who would acknowledge his authority) is not to seek a separation.

IS AN ABANDONED BELIEVER FREE TO REMARRY?

One verse in this discussion has been taken to permit divorce and remarriage. In discussing mixed marriages, Paul instructs,

But if the unbeliever departs, let him depart. The brother or sister is not enslaved in such cases (1 Cor 7:15a).

Some people conclude that not being enslaved means that the believer is free to remarry. This position is reinforced by some translations. They describe the state of the abandoned believer using the verb "*bound*" (RSV, NIV, NET) or the noun "*bondage*" (KJV, ASV, NASB). Then they describe the condition of a widow in verse 39 using the same or a similar English word:

The wife is bound by the law as long as her husband liveth; but if her husband be dead, she is at liberty to be married to whom she will; only in the Lord (1 Cor 7:39, KJV).

Readers of these translations might conclude that since "*bound*" describes the marriage relation in verse 39, and that since death breaks that bond and allows remarriage, someone who is no longer *"bound"* for another reason (verse 15) is also free to remarry.

There are two problems with this interpretation. First, Paul would be reversing the teaching of the Lord Jesus, who allows remarriage only if one spouse is dead. Yet he quotes the Lord, and elsewhere condemns those who differ from the Lord's teaching. Second, the interpretation is based on a false identification of two words. In spite of common English translations, the Greek words in verse 15 and verse 39 are distinct.

In verse 39, *"bound"* (Greek *deō*) is the same verb that Paul uses in Romans 7:2 in a similar context:

*The woman who is under a husband is **bound** by the Law to her living husband. But if her husband should die, she is released from the law of her husband.*

The concrete sense of this verb is "to bind or tie." The death of one spouse unties this bond, dissolves the union, and leaves the survivor free to remarry.

The verb in 1 Corinthians 7:15 is a different verb (Greek *douloō*), meaning literally "to enslave." This verse is the only place in the Bible that the word describes marriage. In other contexts, this second verb and related words emphasize that one person submits to, obeys, and seeks the pleasure of another. For example, Paul describes himself as *"a slave (doulos) of Jesus Christ"* in Romans 1:1, and urges believers to *"present your members slaves to righteousness unto holiness"* (Rom 6:19). In 1 Corinthians 7:15, the word recalls the mutual care of husband and wife in a healthy marriage. It emphasizes the daily duties of marriage, not the "marriage bond." When the unbeliever walks out of a marriage, these duties end for the believer. If an unbelieving wife leaves, her husband does not need to keep her car running. If an unbelieving husband leaves, his wife does not need to consult him on major decisions.

Let's summarize the point of 1 Corinthians 7:15. When the unbeliever departs, the believer is no longer enslaved to the unbeliever. The human duties end. But the verse says nothing about the marriage bond that God has forged. Verse 39 does discuss that bond, using a different Greek word to describe a unity that it then says ends with death. Paul uses different terms in the two verses, so we should not assume that they describe the same concept.

DOES PAUL ALLOW DIVORCE AND REMARRIAGE?

Contrary to popular opinion, 1 Corinthians 7 is not an endorsement of bachelors and old maids. It recognizes both celibacy and marriage as distinct gifts from God to different people. It commands believing couples to stay together, and urges people married to unbelievers to do all they can to preserve their marriages. Paul reinforces the instruction that the Lord Jesus gave his disciples.

When we understand the chapter in this way, verse 15 takes on a new light. It does not define the end of the marriage bond. It simply recognizes that if an unbeliever seeks a separation, the believer may not be able to do anything about it. When the human union is broken, the believer can no longer perform the duties of marriage. An abandoned believer is no longer enslaved to the departed spouse. But such a believer may not remarry, for only death breaks the bond that unites man and wife before God.

6
GOD KNOWS THE WAY OUT

Throughout the Bible, the law of marriage is unchanging. The Bible opens in a garden where man learns that his wife is indivisibly part of him, bone of his bones and flesh of his flesh (Gen 2:23). It closes with the vision of a heavenly paradise from which fornicators are excluded (Rev 22:15). In between, as the longer book shows, every witness agrees that divorce is wrong and remarriage is adultery.

Modern people do not like absolutes. We prefer to hang loose, to remain flexible, to keep our options open. Like rats in a maze, we cannot see the overall problem. We must try one route, then another, hoping to stumble onto a solution. Today's wisdom insists, "Never say 'Never.'" We are loath to accept absolute rules, lest they lead us to a dead end.

Perhaps, in the light of this modern caution, we should relax the conclusions we have reached about divorce and remarriage. Can God's Word really be as inflexible as it seems? Have we read something wrong? Are there really no exceptions, no special cases, no bending of the rules?

This modern attitude has ancient roots. The Jewish leaders of our Lord's day waver on the absolute standards of the Old Testament. They know what the law requires, but tend to compromise, adopting the Greek and Roman practice of divorce. Our Lord calls them back to the absolute standard set forth by Moses.

God's Law seems unrealistic only if we impose human limits on God himself. In fact, God created our world, so he stands outside and above its complexity. He sees the problems and knows the answer. To help us in our dilemma, he speaks to us in the Bible and through his Son (Heb 1:1, 2). He tells us the way out of the maze.

God not only knows our dilemmas better than we do; he can change them. The Bible abounds with examples of mazes whose walls shift at the last moment. God's people, to all appearances trapped beyond hope, suddenly find before them an open door. His enemies, despite their careful plans, find themselves cut off without recourse.

Consider two contrasting examples from the Old Testament, where people face the question of whether or not to obey an outlandish command from God.

Ahab, king of Israel, is a shrewd man. With his advisors, he decides to mount a military campaign against Syria. He persuades Jehoshaphat, the king of Judah, to accompany him. Jehoshaphat asks that they first seek the Lord's instruction, because a military venture is a maze of the worst sort. The adversary is intelligent, the payoff is uncertain, and the risks are high. Jehoshaphat wants to know what the maze looks like from heaven's perspective.

Ahab's court prophets give him the answer he wants:

Go up, and the Lord will give [Ramoth-Gilead] into the king's hand (1 Kings 22:6).

Jehoshaphat suspects their motives, and asks for a second opinion. Through Micaiah the son of Imlah, God announces that the campaign will end in Ahab's death (1 Kings 22:17-23).

Ahab faces a decision. He can heed God's warning, but then he will insult his court prophets, and appear frightened before his own army. Such a show of weakness could invite a coup. Another option is to hope that God's warning is not absolute. Perhaps God only means to point out the danger of the mission. Surely, if Ahab takes special precautions, he can escape death.

Ahab trusts in his cleverness rather than in God's Word. He persuades Jehoshaphat to wear royal robes into battle, and disguises himself to avoid recognition (1 Kings 22:30). But a

Syrian soldier shoots off an arrow at random, and it finds its way between the joints of Ahab's armor, where even the most skilled marksman would not be able to guide it (1 Kings 22:34). By evening, Ahab is dead.

Ahab follows the way of modern man. His world is complex — too complex, certainly, to be comprehended by the simple absolute revelations of God. After all, what does the Lord know about military strategies, or the politics of king and court? He hears God just as much as he pleases, but no more. Then he makes his own decisions and guides his own fate — or so he thinks, until the path that seemed to promise a way out of the maze ends with a stray arrow.

How different is the campaign on which Moses leads Israel out of Egypt. Moses is just as human as Ahab, as we see in his reluctance before the burning bush (Exod 3 and 4). In the end, he accepts his commission. God sends him to Pharaoh with a simple command: "*Let my people go*" (Exod 5:1).

Moses is no stranger to Pharaoh's court. He was raised there, as the son of Pharaoh's daughter. He knows that outright demands are no way to win favors from an oriental despot. Perhaps Moses should just ask for a few tribes. And a command from a God worshipped by slaves is not likely to motivate the Egyptian king. Moses would do much better to say that they need to relieve crowding in the barracks. But God's command allows no such finessing.

> *You shall say to Pharaoh, "Thus says the LORD:*
> *Israel is my son, my firstborn. And I say to you, 'Let*
> *my son go, that he may serve me. And if you refuse to*
> *let him go, behold, I will slay your son, your*
> *firstborn'"* (Exod 4:22, 23).

Moses carries the message as God commands, and Pharaoh responds as we expect. He not only refuses to grant Moses' request, but increases the slaves' load to distract them from any further foolishness. It seems to Moses and the elders of Israel that God has driven them into a dead end. But God patiently responds, *"Now you shall see what I will do to Pharaoh"* (Exod 6:1). And he proceeds to unleash the ten plagues on the land of Egypt.

Eventually Pharaoh relents, and the people pack up to leave. The Lord guides them along a route that leads to the shores of the Red Sea. Then Pharaoh, humiliated at having given in, leads his army out against the fleeing slaves. When the Israelites find the sea before them and the Egyptians at their heels, they criticize Moses. Why did he have to be so dogmatic about God's command to leave Egypt? Couldn't he just have interpreted it as a promise of spiritual freedom? If only he hadn't taken God so literally, they wouldn't be up against this dead end.

By now, Moses has learned that God leads his people into dead ends to show them his power. He replies,

> *Don't be afraid. Take your stand, and see the salvation*
> *of the LORD, which he will perform for you today. ...*
> *The LORD shall fight for you; and as for you, you*
> *shall be quiet* (Exod 14:13, 14).

How dare they suggest that he should not follow God's instruction? God has led them into this dilemma. He will lead them out.

And lead them out he does. A path opens through the Red Sea. Israel marches across on dry land, and when the Egyptian host tries to pursue them, God buries them beneath the waters. To this day, both Jew and Christian remember the victory at the Red Sea. It happened only because Moses was not afraid to let God lead the nation into a dead end, and as a result God's power was displayed.

Where is the way of Ahab? It surrounds us on every side. There are many who say of God's marriage law, "That's too absolute, too inflexible. We know a better way." They try to bend God's revelation, trusting more in their own myopic view of the maze than in the overall perspective that he gives. They agree that, in general, marriage should be permanent. But they think they know enough to make some exceptions to God's rules.

Sadly, they are not wise enough to avoid the arrows from which God could have spared them.

Where is the God of Moses? He is still here, too. He still gives his people instructions, as he did to Moses. Sometimes those instructions seem just as foolish and inflexible as did God's commission for Moses. Yet that commission led straight into a miracle.

Marriage abounds with dead ends: a couple who cannot agree on how to manage their money; a husband who beats his wife; a woman who abandons her believing husband and their children; a newly-saved divorcee who longs for the fellowship of a Christian home. We try to find our way out of the maze ourselves. We allow a divorce here, a remarriage there, not as violations of the biblical law, but as justifiable exceptions to the rule. Ahab's arrow warns that this way leads to God's judgment.

"Impossible" problems show that God intends to make us part of a miracle. Just when the path seems most completely blocked, he says to us, as he said to Moses, *"Now you shall see what I will do."* Sometimes he works quickly; sometimes slowly. But he will work, if only we will obey him and trust him.

Don't be afraid. Take your stand, and see the salvation of the LORD, which he will perform for you today (Exod 14:13).

Appendix 1:
METHODOLOGICAL NOTES

This study focuses on the Scripture text itself, not the comments of others about the text. So I cite almost no "authorities." The longer book cites more, but still very few. Other students may have drawn some of my conclusions. These results are, however, unfamiliar among evangelical believers today, and I am more concerned to publicize them than to trace their history.

The study is based on the Hebrew and Greek texts of the Bible, not only on translations. I follow the Massoretic text of the Old Testament as presented in *Biblia Hebraica Stuttgartensia*, and the majority text in the New Testament as reconstructed in Hodges and Farstad 1982. The English translations are my own. In public exposition, I routinely use the KJV, because of its close approximation to the majority text in the New Testament, its formal rather than dynamic approach to translation, and its preservation of the often critical distinction between singular and plural in the second person in both Hebrew and Greek, and so I will sometimes adopt its wording, gently modernized, in passages where I have no improvements to suggest, but in every case I accept responsibility for the rendering presented. My translations frequently emphasize specific exegetical points, and are not intended to compete with standard translations of the Bible.

Textual variants do not affect the main conclusions reached, and readers who prefer other texts should find the arguments unaffected (though the arguments will be much harder to follow in a translation based on dynamic equivalence).

The discussion frequently refers to the Septuagint ("the Seventy"), abbreviated "the LXX." The LXX is an ancient Jewish translation of the Hebrew Old Testament into Greek. The name comes from a legend that it was prepared by seventy scholars. It was translated before the first century, and the New Testament writers frequently quote it, just as modern Bible teachers usually quote their favorite English version rather than the underlying Hebrew or Greek. The LXX provides a bridge between the Hebrew vocabulary of the Old Testament and the Greek vocabulary of the New Testament.

To understand how this bridge works, let's consider an example in English. In discussing salvation, Christians make frequent use of terms like "redemption," "sanctification," and "propitiation." Where do we get these words, and how do we understand their meaning? They do not occur in the (Greek) New Testament or (Hebrew) Old Testament. But they are the words used in our English Bibles to translate the Greek words that the apostles used in explaining our Lord's work. A responsible discussion of the English word "redemption," for example, must recognize that its meaning comes from its use to translate a specific set of Greek and Hebrew words in the Bible.

Just so, when we are studying a Greek word in the New Testament, we must remember that the authors know the LXX as intimately as we know our English Bible, and often use Greek words in the sense that they have in the LXX, based on the underlying Hebrew.

When I refer to "the Greek Bible," I mean the LXX and the New Testament together.

I sometimes describe imaginary marriage scenarios involving couples like Ann and Andy, or Betty and Bob. These scenarios are fictitious, and any resemblance between the characters in these scenarios and real people is completely coincidental.

To keep this book short, I concentrate on explaining the biblical passages that present our Lord's teaching on the subject. The longer book, available for free at the web site given in the preface, provides detailed discussions of a number of practical questions, including those who are already divorced and remarried, the role of the divorced person in the church, and the problem of physical abuse. The Scriptures do offer guidance on these issues, but the fundamental issue, and the focus of our discussion here, is whether divorce, or subsequent remarriage, is ever justified in the first place.

Appendix 2:
WHAT IS FORNICATION?

Matthew's record of our Lord's teaching on divorce assumes that one spouse is guilty of something called "fornication." What does this term describe? How does it differ from other kinds of sexual conduct condemned by the Bible, such as incest, prostitution, adultery, or homosexual behavior? We are particularly interested in its relationship to adultery, which describes intimacy between a married person and someone other than the other spouse.

To understand the different answers to this question, we need to clarify some distinctions that are used in studying meaning in language. When two different words describe related concepts, they can be related in different ways. We can illustrate these different relationships by comparing the word "dog" with the words "cat" and "mammal."

– "Dog" and "cat" are mutually exclusive. If something is a dog, it cannot be a cat, and *vice versa*.

– In contrast, "mammal" and "dog" are not mutually exclusive. Every dog is also a mammal, as is every cat. However, not every mammal is a dog or a cat. Other mammals include squirrels, ferrets, and whales.

(We are discussing what a linguist calls the extensional meaning of a noun, that is, the set of things to which it applies. The study of meaning also includes intensional meaning, which is defined by the concept to which a word refers. For our purposes, we need only consider extensional meaning.)

These examples illustrate two alternative relations that have been proposed between "fornication" and "adultery." (Many of these interpretations are conveniently documented by Heth 1982.)

Some people understand fornication and adultery to be two distinct kinds of sexual sin, just as dogs and cats are two different kinds of animal. The usual contrast is that fornication involves unmarried people, while adultery requires that one of the people in the sinful union be married (to somebody other than their partner in sin). This distinction is invoked by people who understand the fornication clause to deal with a woman who is found not to be a virgin on her marriage night, as envisioned in Deuteronomy 22:13, 14. Those who understand "fornication" in this way say that the Lord allows a husband to annul such a marriage. It rests on a deception, and so is not legally valid. Thus understood, the clause justifies annulment, but not divorce.

Another contrast that has been proposed is that the fornication clause refers to incest, specifically, the degrees of marriage forbidden in Leviticus 18. This position is usually based on the rule established by the conference in Jerusalem in Acts 15:20, in which Gentiles were urged to "abstain from … fornication" in order not to offend Jews unnecessarily. Again, the Lord's words would authorize annulment of an illegal marriage, not dissolving a legitimate one.

These two suggestions both understand "fornication" to refer to specifically Jewish legislation, and so explain why only Matthew, the most distinctly Jewish of the Gospels, includes the fornication clause. However, they also require Matthew's readers to understand "fornication" as a technical term for a specific kind sexual sin, distinct from other sins such as adultery.

Other interpretations understand "fornication" to be a general term that includes all sexual sin, and "adultery" to be a specific kind of fornication, a relationship between a married person and someone other than that person's spouse. In this case, the relation is like that between "mammal" and "dog." All dogs are mammals, but some mammals are not dogs; all adultery is fornication, but some instances of fornication are not adultery.

Some interpreters think the Lord uses "fornication" to refer to the "matter of uncleanness" described in Deuteronomy 24:1. In this case, "fornication" is just a general designation for any sexual sin. This interpretation lies behind the traditional position as well. Based on Matthew's exception for *fornication*, the Westminster Confession authorizes separation for *adultery*. This reasoning makes sense only if adultery is a form of fornication.

The biblical use of the word "fornication" is decidedly in favor of understanding fornication as a general term and adultery as a specific kind of fornication. The underlying Greek word for fornication and its relatives (the noun *pornē* "harlot," the adjective *pornikos* "pertaining to a harlot," and the verbs *porneuō* and *ekporneuō* "commit fornication, play the harlot") are used in the Bible to describe a wide range of illicit behaviors.

When the LXX wants to describe prostitution, it most often draws from this family of words. Clearly, the sin of prostitution does not apply only to unmarried people, or only to incestuous relations. It is a vehicle for any form of illegitimate union.

Based on the use of these words to describe prostitution, some might suggest that the Bible condemns only commercial impurity, not other relations among people who are not married to one another. This distinction is not supported by the data. A common metaphor in the Old Testament presents the nation Israel as the wife of the Lord, and condemns her idolatry as spiritual fornication. Ezekiel 16:26, 29 uses these words of the nation, even though she did not charge for her services, verses 31-34.

All adultery is fornication, but some instances of fornication are not adultery, because the people involved are not married. A good example is Hosea 4:14,

> *I will not punish your daughters*
> *   when they commit fornication,*
> *nor your daughters in law*
> *   when they commit adultery.*

Hosea's use of the two words in this verse is influenced by the structure of Hebrew poetry. The basic unit of Hebrew poetry is a pair of lines that use different terms with closely related meanings. Here Hosea pairs "daughter" with "daughter in law," and "fornication" with "adultery." It is appropriate for him to accuse a (virgin) daughter of fornication and a (married) daughter in law of adultery, but his usage does not show that the two are as distinct as dogs and cats. The relation between a more general term (fornication) and a more specific one (adultery) fits just as well, and the rules of Hebrew poetry require that he use a different but related word in the second line.

Ezekiel 16 shows that adultery is a specific kind of fornication, not distinct from it. The chapter frequently uses the "fornication" family of words to describe Judah's idolatry, all the while characterizing her as the wife of the Lord. In fact, after repeated descriptions of her sin as fornication, 16:32 describes her as "a wife that commits adultery."

Fornication can have an even broader meaning. Jude 7 uses the term to describe the characteristic sin of Sodom and Gomorrah, which according to the record in Genesis 19 was homosexual rape. The Damascus document (CD), an extra-biblical Hebrew text used at Qumran around the first century, uses a common Hebrew equivalent of the Lord's word for fornication to describe polygamy (zənût, the Hebrew original behind nine of the instances of *porneia* in the LXX), and perhaps incest and other sexual impurity. CD 4.20 clearly links the word to polygamy. Fitzmyer 1976 understands the scope of the saying to extend to 5.6-10, which refer to lying with a woman during her period and incestuous relations as well. The extension is rhetorically questionable, since the text goes on to discuss non-sexual sins such as impious speech (5.11-12), but the broad scope of zənût would certainly make the allusion possible in the mind of the writer.

We conclude that "fornication" is a general word for any kind of sexual sin. Adultery, homosexual acts, polygamy, and incest, as well as premarital relations, are all called "fornication" in the Bible and other Jewish literature of the first century. Given this broad usage, our Lord's words in Matthew would be very misleading if he intended to allow divorce only in a specific technical situation such as incest or impurity before marriage. He chose the broadest term possible, and did not explain it in any way. The broad scope of "fornication" means that his words authorize dismissal for any sexual impurity. We cannot evade their force (or the paradoxes they introduce) by trying to restrict the meaning of "fornication." The word is a very general one, applicable to a wide range of lapses of purity. Certainly, it *includes* incest and premarital dalliances, but it can hardly be *restricted* to these senses.

BIBLIOGRAPHY

ABBREVIATIONS

ASV: The American Standard Version of the Bible
BHS: The Hebrew Old Testament, in the edition of Elliger, K., and W. Rudolph, eds., 1977. *Biblia Hebraica Stuttgartensia*. Stuttgart: Deutsche Bibelstiftung.
CD: The Damascus Document
KJV: The King James Version of the Bible
LXX: The Septuagint, in the edition of A. Rahlfs, 1935. *Septuaginta* . Stuttgart: Württembergische Bibelanstalt / Deutsche Bibelgesellschaft.
NASB: The New American Standard Bible
NET: The New English Translation of the Bible
NIV: The New International Version of the Bible
RSV: The Revised Standard Version of the Bible

OTHER REFERENCES

Fitzmyer, J.A., 1976. "The Matthean Divorce Texts and Some New Palestinian Evidence." *Theological Studies* 37, 197-226.
Heth, William A., 1982. "An Analysis and Critique of the Evangelical Protestant View of Divorce and Remarriage." ThM Thesis, Dallas Theological Seminary, Dallas, TX.
Heth, William A., and Gordon J. Wenham, 1984. *Jesus and Divorce*. London: Hodder and Stoughton.

Hodges, Z.C., and A.L. Farstad, eds., 1982. *The Greek New Testament According to the Majority Text*. Nashville: Thomas Nelson.

Topics and Persons Index

Abimelech....................................47

Achish.......................................47

Adultery......... 1ff., 9, 11, 23, 26ff. 35ff., 49f., 53, 63, 73ff.

Ahab.................................. 64ff.

Antigone.................................. 48

Apocrypha.................................. 47

Arab custom..............................22

Aristotle....................................49

ASV..59

Avenger of blood....................35f.

Babylonian Talmud............. 28, 38

Biblia Hebraica Stuttgartensia. 69

Caesar.. 10

Celibacy................. 52, 54, 56f., 61

Certificate of divorce....... 29f., 36 42ff., 50

Diodorus Siculus........................ 47

Diogenes Laertius.......................48

Dionysius of Halicarnassus..... 47

Dismissed woman.......1f., 5ff., 50

Dynamic equivalence............... 69

Erasmus................. 2ff., 9, 11, 13f.

Execution............................. 28, 35

Farstad, A. L..............................69

Fornication.......... 1ff., 11, 13f., 17 24, 26ff., 39, 46, 49ff., 54, 56, 73ff.

Galilee......................................9

Greek.........2, 5, 27, 42, 45ff., 60f. 63, 69f., 75

Hebrew... 2, 32, 42, 45ff., 69f., 76

Herod Antipas........................ 9, 43

Herodians................................ 10

Heth, William A.................. 14, 74

Hillel...9f., 38

Hodges, Z. C............................. 69

Impurity.........14, 20, 22, 26ff., 36 38, 41, 46, 51, 75ff.

Incest............................73f., 76f.

Jehoshaphat.............................. 64

Jerusalem................................ 9, 74

Jewish custom........................... 22

John the Baptist......................... 9

Jordan river................................ 9

Judah...............................37, 64, 76

King Creon................................48

KJV..............................2, 30, 59, 69

Law of Moses.....3, 14f., 17, 23ff. 36, 38f., 58

Lex Iulia..................................... 28

LXX (see also Septuagint)........27 42, 44ff., 70, 75f.

Lyco... 49

Massoretic text........................... 69

Messiah..........................10, 25, 48

Micaiah the son of Imlah.........64

Mishna..28

Moses.........3, 14f., 17, 22ff., 34ff. 38f., 42ff., 48, 58, 63, 65ff.

Murder............................. 29, 34ff.

NET...59

NIV...59

Paul........................ 3, 5f., 46, 53ff.

Perea.....................................9, 42

Pharaoh............................. 47, 65f.

Pharisees...... 9ff., 15, 23, 28, 42ff. 49ff., 59

Philistines....................................47

Physical abuse............................71

Poll tax......................................10

Prostitution............................ 73, 75

Ramoth-Gilead..............................64

Remarriage....1f., 6ff., 11, 14f., 30
  33ff., 46, 50, 53, 58ff., 63, 67, 71

RSV...59

Septuagint (see also LXX)........70

Shammai.......................9ff., 38, 51

Sophocles......................................48

Stoning...................22, 27, 46, 49f.

Textual variants............................69

Theophrastus.............................. 49

Tokens of virginity....................22

Unbelieving spouse............... 57ff.

Uncleanness........... 30, 38f., 49, 75

Wenham, Gordon J....................14

Westminster Confession.......2, 75

SCRIPTURE INDEX

OLD TESTAMENT

Genesis 2:23.............................. 63
Genesis 3...................................43
Genesis 9:6............................. 35
Genesis 15:2........................... 47
Genesis 19............................... 76
Exodus 3.................................. 65
Exodus 4.................................. 65
Exodus 4:14..............................66
Exodus 4:22..............................65
Exodus 4:23..............................65
Exodus 5:1................................65
Exodus 6:1................................66
Exodus 14:13...................... 66, 67
Leviticus 18..............................74
Leviticus 18:20........................ 33
Leviticus 18:24........................ 33
Leviticus 18:30........................ 33
Numbers 5:11-31.....................36
Numbers 20:28-29.....................47
Numbers 35........................ 35, 36
Numbers 35:31........................ 35
Numbers 35:31-33....................34
Numbers 35:33........................ 35
Deuteronomy 19:12.................. 35
Deuteronomy 19:15.................. 23
Deuteronomy 22...........14, 17, 46
Deuteronomy 22:13.................. 74
Deuteronomy 22:13-21...... 18, 21
                                   22, 36
Deuteronomy 22:13-29...... 17, 21
     26-30, 38, 41, 46, 49, 50, 51
Deuteronomy 22:14.............22, 74
Deuteronomy 22:15-19...... 21, 24

Deuteronomy 22:19.................. 25
Deuteronomy 22:20-21...... 21, 24
Deuteronomy 22:22............19, 21
                                   23, 24
Deuteronomy 22:23-24...... 19, 21
.... 23, 24
Deuteronomy 22:23-27...... 22, 25
Deuteronomy 22:25-2720, 21, 24
Deuteronomy 22:28-29...... 20, 21
                               22, 24, 25
Deuteronomy 22:29.................. 25
Deuteronomy 24...........14, 35, 45
Deuteronomy 24:1........ 30-33, 36
                           42, 44, 46, 75
Deuteronomy 24:1-3.................32
Deuteronomy 24:1-4........... 29-34
                             37-39, 41-46
Deuteronomy 24:1-4a.............. 31
Deuteronomy 24:2........30, 31, 32
                                      45
Deuteronomy 24:3.....................32
Deuteronomy 24:3-4................. 30
Deuteronomy 24:3-4a.............. 31
Deuteronomy 24:4............. 32, 34
Deuteronomy 24:4a....................32
Deuteronomy 24:4b............31, 34
Deuteronomy 29:29.................. 26
1 Samuel 2:6............................. 52
1 Samuel 21:10-22:1................. 47
1 Kings 22:6............................64
1 Kings 22:17-23......................64
1 Kings 22:30.......................... 64
1 Kings 22:34.......................... 65
Ezra 9-10................................58
Psalm 33:1...............................46

Psalm 34 46
Jeremiah 3:1............................34, 37
Jeremiah 3:9.............................35
Ezekiel 16:26.............................75
Ezekiel 16:29.............................75
Ezekiel 16:31-34.........................75
Hosea 4:14.................................75
Malachi 2:10.............................25
Malachi 2:16.............................50

APOCRYPHA

1 Esdras 9:36.............................47

NEW TESTAMENT

Matthew 1:18.............................24
Matthew 5...................... 1, 27, 51
Matthew 5:17-20................9, 15
Matthew 5:20.............................9
Matthew 5:21.............................8
Matthew 5:22-26.........................8
Matthew 5:27.............................8
Matthew 5:28-30..........................8
Matthew 5:30-32.......................... 5
Matthew 5:31.................. 8, 42, 44
Matthew 5:31-32......... 1, 6, 41, 42
Matthew 5:32..3, 5, 6, 7, 8, 12, 13
           14, 41, 42, 46, 49, 50, 51
Matthew 5:33.............................8
Matthew 5:34-37......................... 8
Matthew 5:38.............................8
Matthew 5:39.............................52
Matthew 5:39-42......................... 8
Matthew 5:43.............................8
Matthew 5:44-48......................... 8
Matthew 19......... 1, 10, 27, 56, 57

Matthew 19:3.............................10
Matthew 19:3-9.......................... 42
Matthew 19:4-6......................... 10
Matthew 19:7..................... 44, 45
Matthew 19:7-8.......................... 42
Matthew 19:8.............................44
Matthew 19:9..1, 2, 4, 5, 9, 11, 12
           13, 14, 41, 46, 50, 51
Matthew 19:9a............................ 4
Matthew 19:10.............................57
Matthew 19:11.............................57
Matthew 22................................10
Matthew 22:16-17.......................10
Mark 6:17-28............................ 9
Mark 10.................................. 1
Mark 10:2-4............................ 42
Mark 10:5................................43
Mark 10:6-9............................ 43
Mark 10:10-12.......................... 1
Mark 10:11.............................. 4
Mark 10:11-12.......................11, 12
Luke 2:29-30.............................48
Luke 12:13............................. 10
Luke 12:14............................. 10
Luke 16...................................1
Luke 16:17-18............................1
Luke 16:18........................ 5, 12
John 8:1-11............................ 23
John 8:2-11............................ 27
John 8:3-5................................23
John 8:10-11........................... 23
John 18:36................................27
John 21:25................................13
Acts 15:20.............................. 74
Romans 1:1.............................. 60
Romans 6:19............................. 60
Romans 7:2............................. 60
Romans 13................................27
Romans 13:4..............................52
1 Corinthians 7..............46, 53, 54
                          56, 61

1 Corinthians 7:1...................... 53
1 Corinthians 7:1-2....................54
1 Corinthians 7:1b......................54
1 Corinthians 7:2................. 54, 56
1 Corinthians 7:7................. 56, 57
1 Corinthians 7:8-9....................57
1 Corinthians 7:10..................... 59
1 Corinthians 7:10-11...56, 57, 58
1 Corinthians 7:12..............58, 59
1 Corinthians 7:12-16................57
1 Corinthians 7:13..................... 58
1 Corinthians 7:15..............60, 61
1 Corinthians 7:15a................... 59

1 Corinthians 7:17...............56, 57
1 Corinthians 7:38..................... 53
1 Corinthians 7:39..............60, 61
1 Corinthians 7:40..................... 53
Ephesians 5............................... 54
1 Timothy 4:3.......................54, 55
1 Timothy 5:14..........................54
1 Timothy 6:3-4......................... 56
Hebrews 1:1...............................64
Hebrews 1:2...............................64
Jude 7..76
Revelation 22:15.........................63

Also in the
Areopagus Critical Christian Issues Series

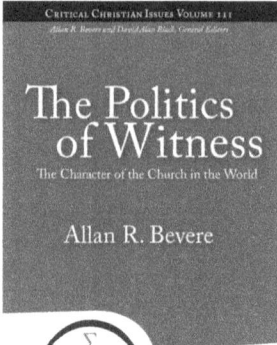

In *The Politics of Witness*, Dr. Allan R. Bevere asks why the church can't speak the truth effectively to power and proposes an answer. The church has come to depend too much on temporal power and has thus forgotten its divine authority. In finding this answer he goes back to the founding of the church and how it first became dependent on the state. He examines those who have followed, mostly building a political theory that takes the responsibility of ministry from the church and gives it to the state.

You'll find some names in this that might surprise you. Any discussion of Christianity and the state will involve Emperor Constantine, but what about his modern lieutenants, such as Locke, Jefferson, Franklin, and others?

While the theology applies to the church in any country, Dr. Bevere takes a particular look at the peculiarly American view that the United States of America is somehow God's chosen people, a nation of destiny in accomplishing the gospel mission.

What is the Kingdom of God? What does it mean to be part of the kingdom? These are questions that should occupy the mind of every Christian. But we frequently shy away from the full meaning of God's rule.

In *Christian Archy*, **Dr. David Alan Black** examines the New Testament to find the truly radical and all-encompassing claims of God's kingdom. In doing so, he discovers that the character of this kingdom is widely different from what is commonly contemplated today. Its glory is revealed only through suffering — a point that Jesus' disciples, then and now, have been slow to understand. This truth has tremendous implications for church life. The kingdom of God is in no way imperialistic. It has no political ambitions. It conquers not by force but by love. It is this humble characteristic of the kingdom that is a stumbling block to so many today. Christ's claim to our total allegiance is one we seek to avoid at all costs. But there is only one way to victory and peace, and that way is the way of the Lamb.

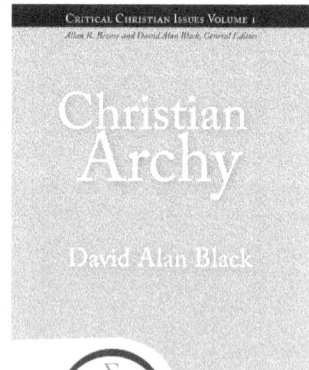

More from Energion Publications

Personal Study

The Jesus Paradigm	$17.99
Finding My Way in Christianity	$16.99
When People Speak for God	$17.99
Holy Smoke, Unholy Fire	$14.99
Not Ashamed of the Gospel	$12.99
Evidence for the Bible	$16.99
Christianity and Secularism	$16.99
What's In A Version?	$12.99
Christian Archy	$9.99
The Messiah and His Kingdom to Come	$19.99 (B&W)

Christian Living

52 Weeks of Ordinary People – Extraordinary God	$7.99
Daily Devotions of Ordinary People – Extraordinary God	$19.99
Directed Paths	$7.99
Grief: Finding the Candle of Light	$8.99
I Want to Pray	$7.99
Soup Kitchen for the Soul	$12.99

Bible Study

Learning and Living Scripture	$12.99
To the Hebrews: A Participatory Study Guide	$9.99
Revelation: A Participatory Study Guide	$9.99
The Gospel According to St. Luke: A Participatory Study Guide	$8.99
Identifying Your Gifts and Service: Small Group Edition	$12.99
Consider Christianity, Volume I & II Study Guides	$7.99 each
Why Four Gospels?	$11.99

Theology

God's Desire for the Nations	$18.99

Fiction

Megabelt	$12.99

Generous Quantity Discounts Available

Dealer Inquiries Welcome

Energion Publications

P.O. Box 841

Gonzalez, FL 32560

Website: http://energionpubs.com

Phone: (850) 525-3916

www.ingramcontent.com/pod-product-compliance
Lightning Source LLC
Chambersburg PA
CBHW051845040426

42447CB00006B/702